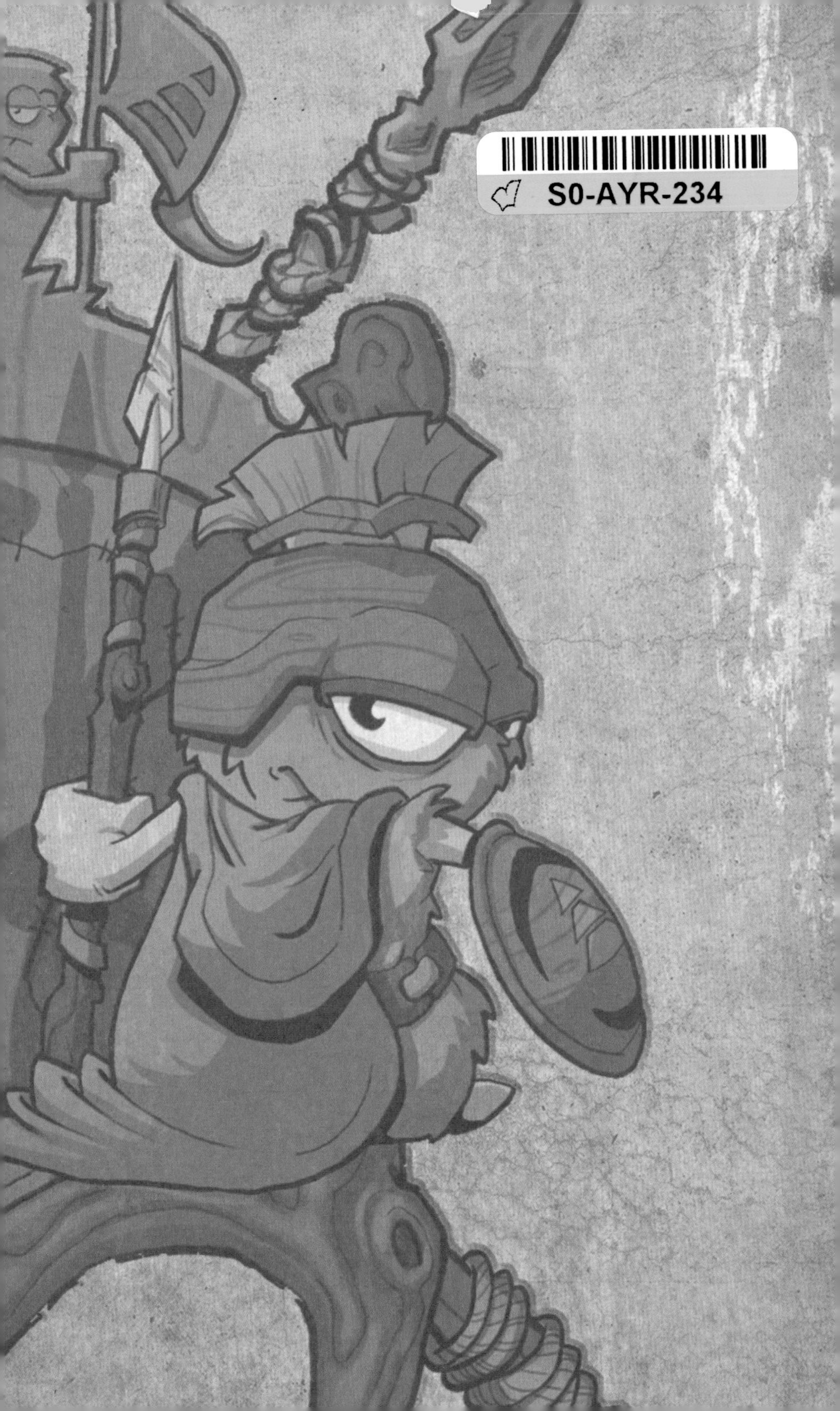

THE WEIGHT IS ON

Archaia Entertainment LLC
WWW.ARCHAIA.COM

JESSE LABBÉ
Story, Color & Cropone Art

Jesse Labbé was born in Biloxi, Mississippi and loves to draw and write stories. He and his wife have intentions of venturing out into the world and have already made plans to relocate to the Krite Forest where they can become one with nature.

ANTHONY COFFEY
Cover, Layout & Ele-Alta Art

Anthony Coffey was born in Odessa, Texas with a pencil in his hand and a song in his heart. This song is now the the great Ele-Alta National Anthem. His utter disdain for the Cropones has led him to sign up for enlistment. He has asperations of becoming one of the great Ele-Alta assassins, but will probably end up being a soil relocation engineer.

Additional Art by WADE ACUFF & JAY SHULTZ

Find the Creators at:

JESSE LABBÉ
www.myspace.com/24080068
www.facebook.com/labbe.enterprise
labbe.enterprise@gmail.com

ANTHONY COFFEY
www.myspace.com/coffeybean4
anthonycoffey@gmail.com

WADE ACUFF
www.wadeacuff.com
www.myspace/com/139044775

JAY SHULTZ
www.myspace.com/doodle_a_day

Book design and layout by Anthony Coffey & Scott Newman

Published by Archaia

Archaia Entertainment LLC
1680 Vine Street, Suite 912
Los Angeles, California, 90028, USA
www.archaia.com

BERONA'S WAR: FIELD GUIDE

August 2010

FIRST PRINTING

10 9 8 7 6 5 4 3 2 1

ISBN: 1-932386-89-0
ISBN 13: 978-1-932386-89-9

ARCHAIA™

Printed in South Korea.

FOREWORD

Jesse and Anthony really have something special on theri hands with *Berona's War*. Every time I browse through my first edition copy, I'm both inspired to create and angry that they have so many great ideas flowing out of them. It doesn't really seem that fair to the rest of us.

This is the spot where a lot of book intros start to get very flowery with the writing or someone starts some story about themselves that has nothing to do with anything, yet will end with being loosely tied to the book they're supposed to be talking about. That won't be happening here. Instead, let's keep it quick and easy so you all can enjoy the following pages.

Berona is a world filled with furry creatures battling hairy creatures in the great tradition of all the beloved fantasy stories that have come before it. Who wants more than that?

Oh, you do? Okay. There are sweet maps, bizarrely fun weapons that will probably do their share of some down and dirty war related activities, and character you'll never want to stop reading about. Jesse and Anthony seemed to have thought of everything and put it all down with pen, ink and pixels for all of us to enjoy.

Simply put, you're about to read a fun book by a few great cartoonists that are proving on every page they are here to have a blast. Let's go join them.

–SKOTTIE YOUNG
June 2010

Skottie Young is the illustrator of the New York Times Best Selling and Eisner Award Nominated adaptions of L. Frank Baum's OZ novels with writer Eric Shanower. The series has gained acclaim from both fans and critics.

I WAS YOUNG WHEN THE WAR STARTED, BUT NOT SO YOUNG THAT I CAN'T REMEMBER HAPPIER DAYS.

THE STORY BEGINS...   -LYNN

THIS IS THE LAND

BERONA ISLAND

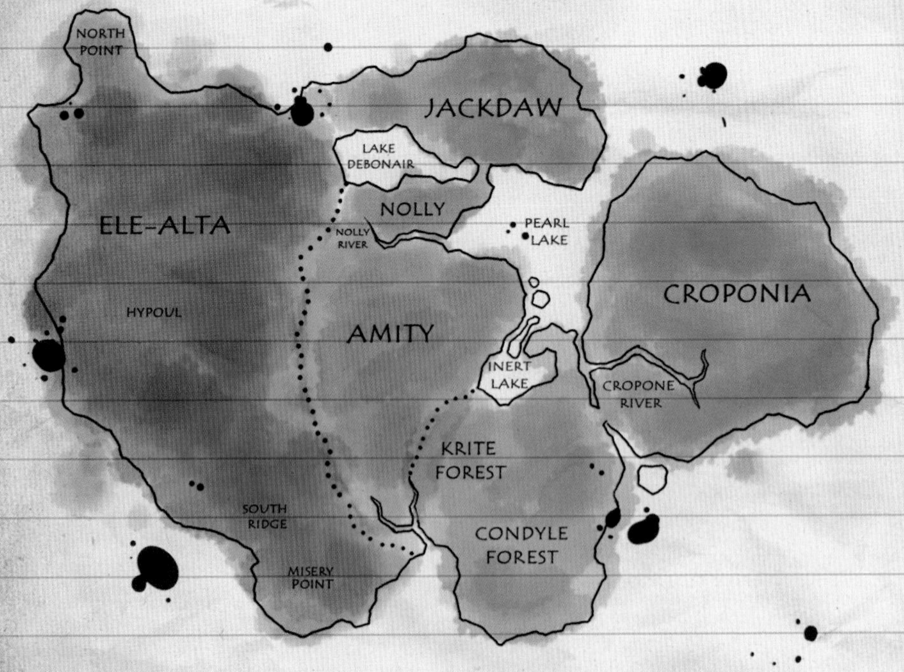
NORTH POINT
JACKDAW
LAKE DEBONAIR
NOLLY
ELE-ALTA
NOLLY RIVER
PEARL LAKE
CROPONIA
HYPOUL
AMITY
INERT LAKE
CROPONE RIVER
KRITE FOREST
SOUTH RIDGE
CONDYLE FOREST
MISERY POINT

TO THE WEST, MOUNTAINOUS LANDS COVERED IN ROCKY TRAILS LEADING TO GRAVEL HILLS AS FAR AS THE EYE CAN SEE.

TO THE EAST, FORESTS AND LUSH JUNGLES AS WELL AS GREEN PLAINS AND GOLDEN FIELDS...A FARMER'S DREAM.

AND SOMEWHERE IN-BETWEEN...IS THE LAND.

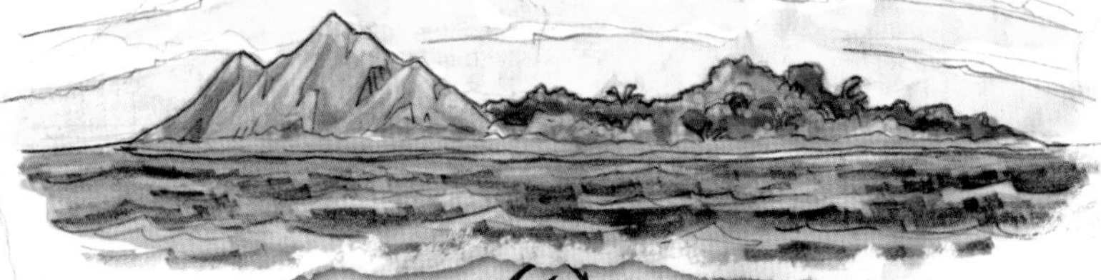

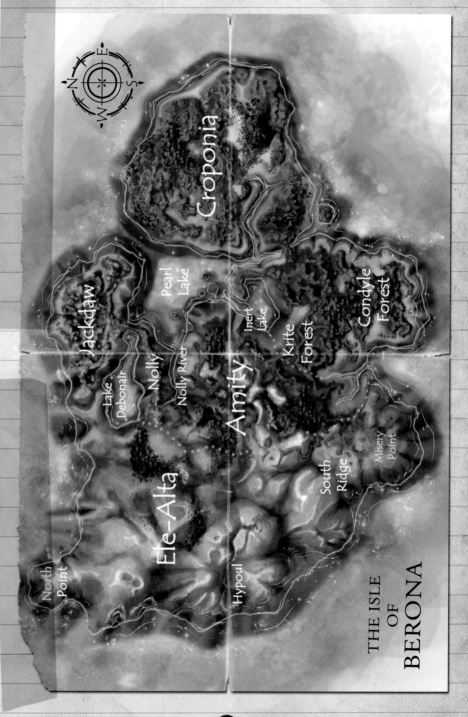

THE ISLE
OF
BERONA

Croponia

Jackdaw

Pearl
Lake

Lake
Debonair

Nolly

Nolly River

Inert
Lake

Krite
Forest

Condyle
Forest

Amity

Ele-Alta

South
Ridge

Misery
Point

North
Point

Hypoul

CRYSTAL CLEAR WATER CONSTANTLY FLOWS FROM ELE-ALTA NORTH POINT.

AMITY IS WHERE GREEN MEETS GREY.

THE ELE-ALTA LIVED FOR WORK. IT WAS THEIR WAY OF LIFE.

AMITY MOUNTAIN

ANCHOR WASP

EFFATOPE — A STONE THAT BECAME MORE AND MORE USEFUL AS THE WAR GREW.

ALMOST ALL WILDLIFE THAT ROAMED THE ISLAND WAS LOCATED IN THE WESTERN CROPONE AREA. MOST OF THE EXOTIC ANIMALS WERE AROUND THE KRITE FOREST.

THE CABBALU

THE ENDANGERED CABBALU FINDS HIMSELF STRUGGLING TO SURVIVE.

MANY SOLDIERS WERE SAID TO HAVE GONE MISSING AFTER ENTERING THE BEAUTIFUL AND DARK LAND OF NOLLY.

CROPONES BELIEVED THE CENTER OF CROPONIA WAS THE HEART OF THE BERONA.

XESIDINE BERRIES ARE INDIGENOUS TO JACKDAW.

9

THIS IS THE GROUP

WHO CLAIMED THE LAND
AND STARTED BERONA'S WAR.

THE CROPONES HAD NO INTENTION OF STARTING A FIGHT,
NOT TO MENTION A WAR, BUT ONCE THEY FOUND
THE PERFECT PIECE OF LAND...IT COULDN'T BE PASSED UP.

CRO-PONE — [KRA-POHN] — (CROP ONE/ONE CROP)

CROPONE: A WELL DISCIPLINED RACE OF CREATURES FROM
THE LAND OF CROPONIA MOSTLY CONSISTING OF FARMERS
LIVING OFF THE GRASSY AND WOODED AREAS OF THE LAND.

LAKE PEARL

CROPONIA

CROPONE RIVER

N
W
E
S

CROPONIANS ARE HIGHLY INTELLIGENT PROBLEM SOLVERS
WITH MANY DIFFERENT BELIEFS. BECAUSE OF THEIR
CONFLICTING VIEWS THE CROPONES WERE EASILY DIVIDED
INTO DIFFERENT GROUPS.

THESE ARE THE WARRIORS

WHO KNEW WHAT THEY WANTED
AND TOOK IT IN BERONA'S WAR.

THE ELE-ALTA ARE THE WORK HORSES OF THE MOUNTAIN RANGE. THEY ARE POWERFUL AND HARD WORKING CREATURES. WORKING IS THEIR WHOLE WAY OF LIFE.

EL-E-AL-TA — [EL-EH-ALL-TUH] — (ELEVATION/ALTITUDE)

UNLIKE THE CROPONES, THE ELE-ALTA ARE NOT DIVIDED INTO DIFFERENT GROUPS. THEY WORK, LIVE, EAT AND THRIVE AS ONE CULTURE. THEY LIVE TO WORK!

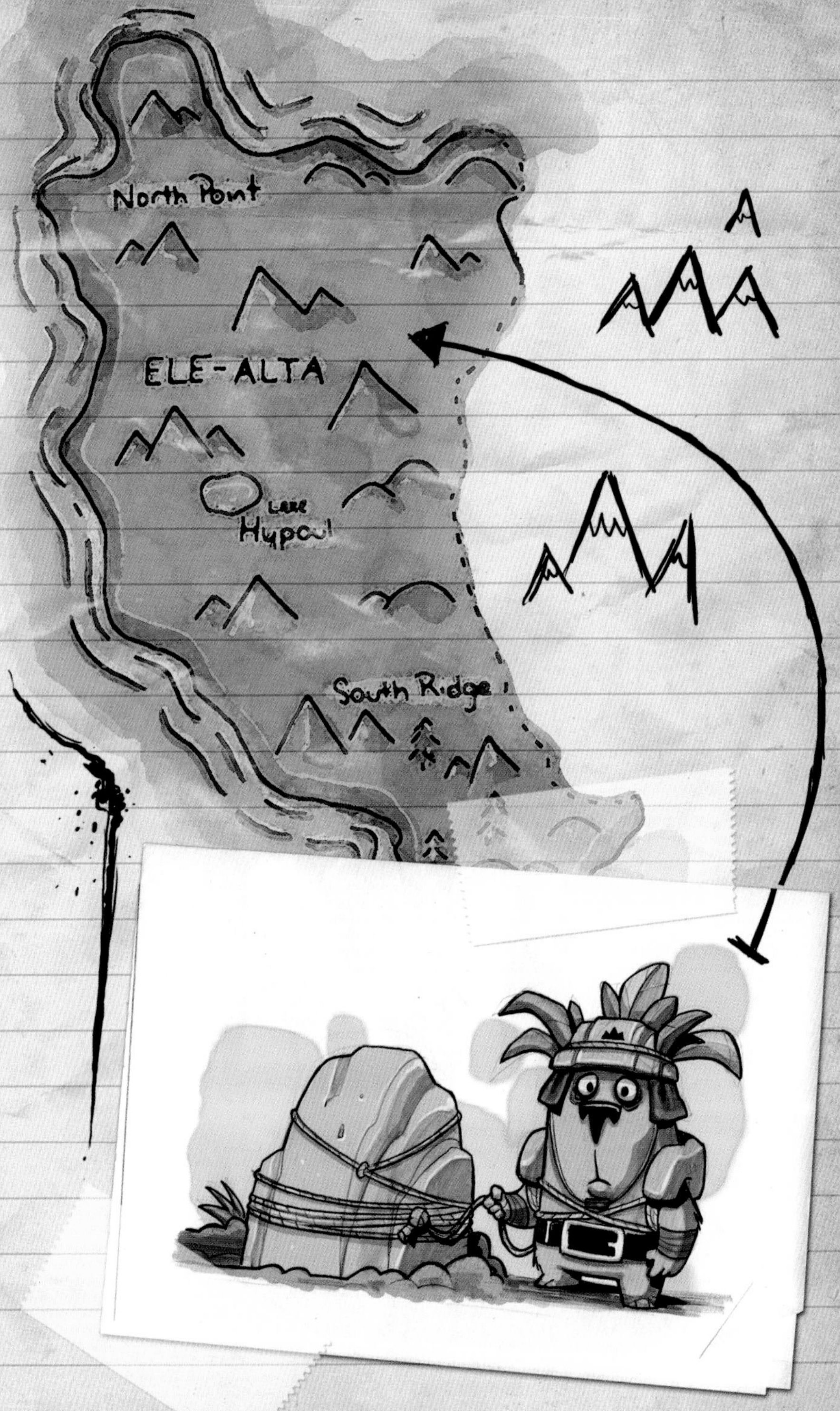
North Point
ELE-ALTA
LAKE
Hypool
South Ridge

THESE ARE THE FIRST

WHO EXCHANGED THE WORDS
THAT EMBITTERED BERONA'S WAR.

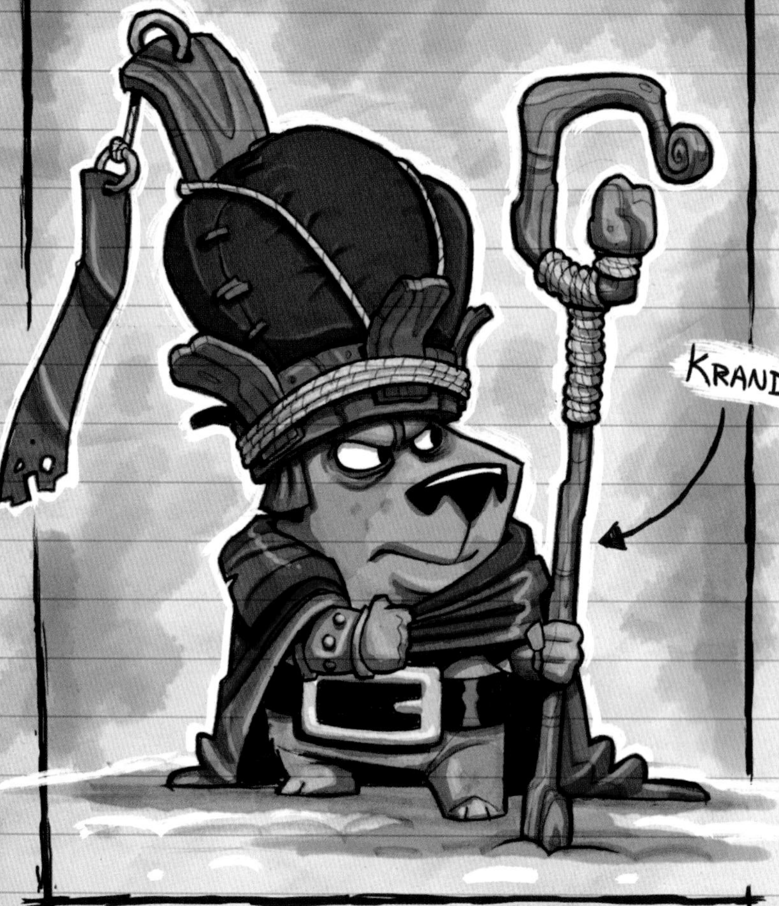
KRAND

IT'S FUNNY HOW SOMETHING SO SIMPLE AS A DISAGREEMENT CAN LEAD TO SOMETHING AS BIG AS A FIGHT, AND HOW A FIGHT CAN LEAD TO A BATTLE, AND A BATTLE CAN LEAD...TO A WAR.

THE ONES WHO WERE OVERSEEING PRODUCTION AND WERE,
FOR THE MOST PART, GOOD, WERE OVERTAKEN QUICKLY BY GREED.

WITH MOST WILLING TO DO ANYTHING TO GAIN
LOYALTY AND RESPECT AMONGST THEIR PEERS,
IT WAS EASY TO FILL THE ROSTER OF WAR.

THIS IS THE DETERMINED

WHO WAS RIGHT UP FRONT
AND LED THE FIRST WAVE IN BERONA'S WAR.

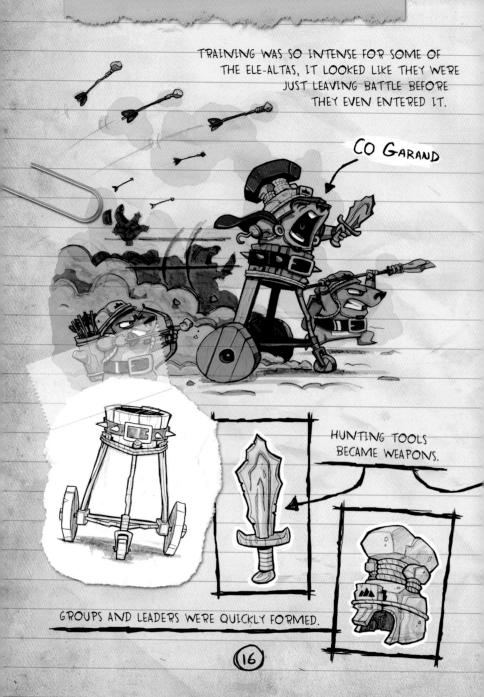

TRAINING WAS SO INTENSE FOR SOME OF
THE ELE-ALTAS, IT LOOKED LIKE THEY WERE
JUST LEAVING BATTLE BEFORE
THEY EVEN ENTERED IT.

CO GARAND

HUNTING TOOLS
BECAME WEAPONS.

GROUPS AND LEADERS WERE QUICKLY FORMED.

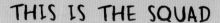

THIS IS THE SQUAD

THAT HELD OFF THE ENEMY AND WAS DUG IN FOR BERONA'S WAR.

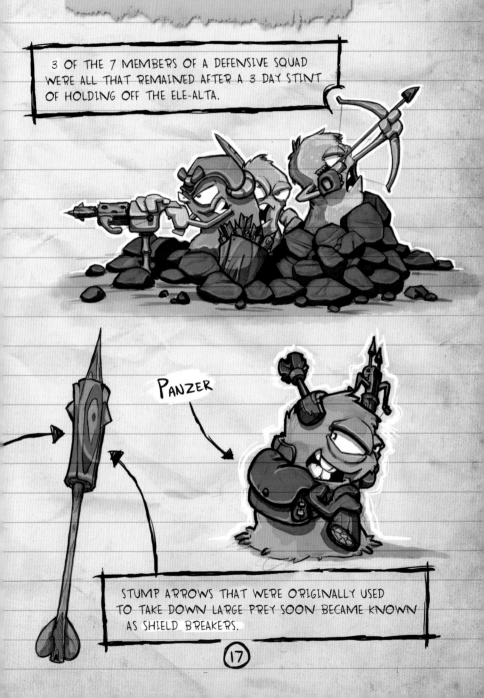

3 OF THE 7 MEMBERS OF A DEFENSIVE SQUAD WERE ALL THAT REMAINED AFTER A 3 DAY STINT OF HOLDING OFF THE ELE-ALTA.

PANZER

STUMP ARROWS THAT WERE ORIGINALLY USED TO TAKE DOWN LARGE PREY SOON BECAME KNOWN AS SHIELD BREAKERS.

THESE ARE THE WATCHMEN

THAT COULD SEE FOR MILES
AND GAVE AN EDGE IN BERONA'S WAR.

WORKERS AND EVEN MEMBERS OF THEIR FAMILIES
SOON TOOK UP POSTS TO WATCH THE LAND FOR
SIGNS OF DANGER

LEITH

BOREDOM SET IN QUICKLY FOR THE LONE CROPONES.

SPECIFIC TOOLS WERE DESIGNED FOR
THE SOLE PURPOSE OF SPOTTING DANGER
QUICKLY.

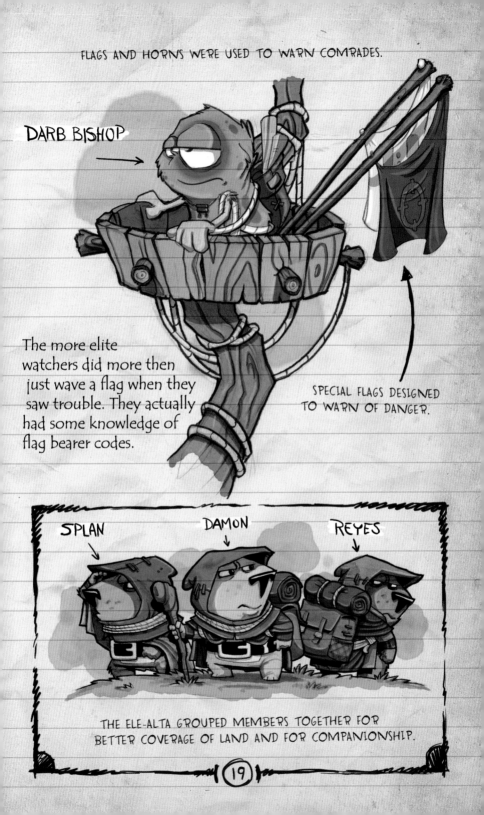

FLAGS AND HORNS WERE USED TO WARN COMRADES.

DARB BISHOP

The more elite watchers did more then just wave a flag when they saw trouble. They actually had some knowledge of flag bearer codes.

SPECIAL FLAGS DESIGNED TO WARN OF DANGER.

SPLAN   DAMON   REYES

THE ELE-ALTA GROUPED MEMBERS TOGETHER FOR BETTER COVERAGE OF LAND AND FOR COMPANIONSHIP.

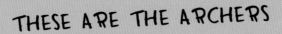

THESE ARE THE ARCHERS

WHO DARKENED THE SKIES
AND WERE CRUCIAL TO BERONA'S WAR.

THE ARCHER WAS THE EASIEST
POSITION TO FILL.

ENFIELD

HUNTERS WHO ALREADY HAD
EXPERIENCE WITH THE BOW
WOULD TEACH OTHERS
HOW TO SHOOT.

REISING

SCOOTER

WHEN THINGS GOT ROUGH, EVEN FEMALES WERE TOLD TO STAND IN THE REAR AND FIRE ON COMMAND

Z

EVEN WITH THE MANY ADVANCEMENTS DURING THE WAR, THE BOW AND ARROW WAS THE MOST USED WEAPON AND WAS RESPONSIBLE FOR MORE THAN HALF OF THE FALLEN.

THESE ARE THE SNIPERS

WHO USED PINPOINT ACCURACY
AND WERE RARELY SPOTTED IN BERONA'S WAR.

ONLY THE HIGHLY TALENTED ARCHERS WERE EVEN
CONSIDERED TO BECOME SNIPERS.

THOUGH THE SNIPERS WERE HIGHLY SKILLED MARKSMEN,
THEY COULD ONLY FIRE ONE ROUND IN THE TIME IT
WOULD TAKE AN AVERAGE ARCHER TO
SHOOT 4 OR 5 QUICK SHOTS.

KRIEG

SNIPERS WERE TRAINED TO FIRE
ON HIGH RANKING OFFICERS,
RUNNERS AND FLAG BEARERS.
NO SNIPER WOULD EVER FIRE
ON A MEDIC. THAT WAS AGAINST
THEIR CODE.

SIMO HAHA

DUE TO THE HIGH LEVEL OF PHYSICAL AND MENTAL DEMANDS, THERE WERE ONLY A HANDFUL OF CROPONES THAT COULD COMMIT TO THE LIFE OF A SNIPER.

THERE ARE STORIES OF SNIPERS STAYING IN ONE LOCATION FOR DAYS, EVEN WEEKS TO WAIT FOR THE PERFECT SHOT...USUALLY RUNNERS OR FLAG BEARERS.

THE NATURAL MARKINGS OF SOME CROPONES MADE THE NEED FOR CAMOUFLAGE HIGHLY UNNECESSARY.

WHITMAN

THIS IS THE M.R.

WHO DUG BEHIND ENEMY LINES AND WERE INVALUABLE IN BERONA'S WAR.

NAMED AFTER THE ROCK MOLE WHICH BURROWS A NETWORK OF TUNNELS IN THE SOIL FOR MATING AND MIGRATION PURPOSES.

AFTER THE SUCCESS OF THE CROPONE SNIPERS, THE ELE-ALTA NEEDED A WAY TO STRIKE BACK...THE MOLE RECON WAS THEIR ANSWER.

GEHLEN

MUCH LIKE THE SNIPERS, THE M.R. WERE ELITE SOLDIERS HAND PICKED FOR THEIR SPECIFIC SKILLS. THEIR JOB WAS TO BURROW ACROSS THE BATTLEFIELD AND RESURFACE BEHIND ENEMY LINES. FROM THERE, THEY COULD RELAY VALUABLE INTELLIGENCE TO THE RUNNERS AND FLAG BEARERS. AND SO THE RIVALRY BETWEEN THE CROPONE SNIPERS AND THE ELE-ALTA M.R. BEGAN.

THE TUNNELS WERE QUICKLY DUG AND LACKED SUFFICIENT SUPPORT STRUCTURES. BECAUSE OF THE DANGEROUS CONDITIONS, THE M.P. WOULD NOT ALLOW OTHER SOLDIERS TO USE THE TUNNELS FOR TRANSPORT.

ZORGE

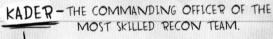

KADER — THE COMMANDING OFFICER OF THE MOST SKILLED RECON TEAM.

THEY SOON DISCOVERED THAT IF HOLES WERE DUG CLOSE ENOUGH TO THE SURFACE, ANY PASSING SOLDIERS WOULD FALL THROUGH THE LOOSE SOIL ONTO WOODED SPIKES SET BELOW.

THESE ARE THE FLAG BEARERS

WHO WERE THE EYES AND EARS
AND SPOKE FOR BERONA'S WAR.

FLAG BEARERS WERE USED BY BOTH
SIDES TO RELAY ORDERS ACROSS
THE BATTLEFIELD. IT WAS QUICKER
TO USE A FLAG BEARER THAN IT
WAS TO SEND A RUNNER
TO A GROUP OUT OF
SHOUTING DISTANCE.

A SINGLE FLAG COULD HAVE SEVERAL DIFFERENT MEANINGS DEPENDING ON THE MANNER IT WAS WAVED. THERE WERE COUNTLESS FLAGS AND COMBINATIONS THAT COULD BE USED, AND IT WAS THE FLAG BEARER'S JOB TO KNOW THEM ALL.

JULIUS

SOME SOLDIERS DREAMED OF NOTHING MORE THAN THE CHANCE TO WAVE A FLAG IN BATTLE.

COOPER

THE FLAG BEARER WAS ARGUABLY ONE OF THE MOST PRESTIGIOUS POSITIONS IN THE WAR.

THESE ARE THE RUNNERS

WHO WERE HIGHLY TARGETED
BUT NEVER QUIT IN BERONA'S WAR.

WHEN A FLAG BEARER COULDN'T GET AN ORDER ACROSS, THE RUNNERS WERE USED TO DELIVER THE MESSAGE.

THE RUNNERS WERE OFTEN TARGETED BY THE ENEMY TO ENSURE MESSAGES WERE NOT DELIVERED. BECAUSE OF THIS, THE RUNNER WAS A TOUGH POSITION TO FILL.

J. BRISBY

RUNNERS HAD SO MUCH RESPECT FOR EACH OTHER THAT IF TWO ENEMY RUNNERS WERE TO COME ACROSS ONE ANOTHER DURING BATTLE, THEY WOULD SHARE FOOD AND SHELTER.

GATLIN

THIS IS THE TRAITOR

WHO WAS EASILY BOUGHT
AND CHANGED SIDES IN BERONA'S WAR.

WITH WAR OVERTAKING THE LAND QUICKLY, FOOD WAS BECOMING SCARCE AND THE EVERYDAY ROUTINE OF LIVING WAS CHANGING RAPIDLY. SOME FOUND THEMSELVES DOING THE UNTHINKABLE.

THE SPY WAS A RUNNER!

HASKELL

LOYALTY, FOR THE MOST PART, WAS A BIG ISSUE WITH BOTH GROUPS...BUT TOUGH TIMES CAN CHANGE ANYONE.

THE SPY WAS GIVING THE ELE-ALTA THE CROPONE FLAG CODES TO BE USED FOR PLANNING COUNTER ATTACKS.

THIS IS WUBS

WHO HAD NO SOUL
AND SHOWED NO MERCY IN BERONA'S WAR.

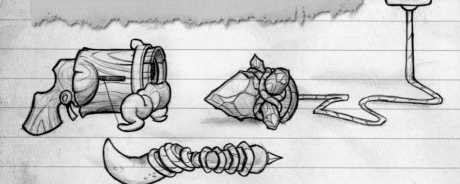

ALTHOUGH THE CROPONES WERE NOT DESIGNED FOR WAR AS WELL AS THEIR OPPONENTS SEEMED TO BE, SOME OF THEM STILL SEEMED TO FEEL AT HOME ON THE BATTLEFIELD.

BEFORE THE WAR THE ABNORMALLY LARGE CROPONE, WUBS, SPENT HIS DAYS CLEARING GIANT ROCKS AND STUMPS FROM FIELDS TO BE USED FOR FARMING. NOW HE IS A FORCE TO BE RECKONED WITH.

THIS IS AN ARMOR-KRIOS

WHICH WAS ONE OF TEN
AND RARELY USED IN BERONA'S WAR.

STONE, THE MOST AVAILABLE RESOURCE FOR THE ELE-ALTA, WAS
USED IN ALMOST ALL TOOLS, WEAPONS, AND EQUIPMENT...BUT
IT DIDN'T SEEM LIKE THE BEST MATERIAL FOR ARMOR. AT LEAST
NOT IN SUCH LARGE AMOUNTS. IT WAS A SOLID IDEA, JUST
POORLY EXECUTED.

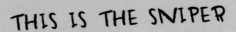

THIS IS THE SNIPER

WHO KILLED THE HEAD M.R.
AND WAS RECOGNIZED IN BERONA'S WAR.

BLUE

ANY FEUD THE SNIPERS AND M.R. MAY HAVE HAD WAS QUICKLY
INTENSIFIED AFTER ONE OF THE CROPONE SNIPERS DECIDED TO
TAKE MATTERS INTO HIS OWN HANDS AND TARGET THE
HEAD OF THE M.R.

THIS IS THE M.R.

WHO KILLED THE HEAD SNIPER AND WAS UNKNOWN IN BERONA'S WAR.

THE MOLE RECON WAS SPECIFICALLY ORDERED NOT TO STRIKE BACK IN FEAR THAT RETALIATION MAY DISTRACT THE SQUAD FROM THEIR PRIMARY OBJECTIVE. ALTHOUGH ONE SOLDIER, BLINDED BY RAGE, DECIEDED TO TAKE MATTERS INTO HIS OWN HANDS.

WHEN THE SOLDIER RESPONSIBLE WAS ASKED TO STEP FORWARD AND ACCEPT THEIR PUNISHMENT, EACH M.R. CONFESSED TO BEING GUILTY. STRONG WAS THE BOND OF THE M.R. JONG, BELIEVED TO BE THE SOLDIER BEHIND THE RETALIATION, WAS NEVER PROVED TO BE RESPONSIBLE.

THIS IS THE CONDYLE

WHO WERE CRUDE AT BEST
BUT SHOWED NO FEAR IN BERONA'S WAR.

ASSAM

IN THE SOUTHERN PART OF CROPONIA LIES A GROUP OF CROPONES WHO ARE LABELED "LESS-CIVILIZED", BUT WHAT THEY LACK IN CULTURE, THEY MAKE UP IN POWER AND PRIDE. THE CONDYLE DIDN'T FOLLOW SUIT WITH THE AVERAGE CROPONE. THEY SHARED FEW SIMILARITIES IN THEIR BELIEFS AS WELL AS THE MANNER IN WHICH THEY LIVED. THEIR VICIOUSNESS ON THE BATTLEFIELD WAS PROOF.

UNTIL THE WAR, THE CROPONES NEVER THOUGHT TOO HIGHLY OF THE CONDYLE. HOWEVER, ONCE ENGAGED IN BATTLE THE CONDYLE GAVE STRENGTH TO ALL THE CROPONE SOLDIERS WHO FOUGHT BY THEIR SIDE.

MOST OF THEIR EQUIPMENT
AND WEAPONS WERE MADE FROM BONE.

INSPIRATION FOR THE CROPONE SOLDIERS' CHEST PLATES WAS TAKEN FROM THE CONDYLE.

ALTHOUGH OUTDATED, THE SHAMAN WERE STILL A LARGE PART OF THE CONDYLE BELIEF SYSTEM AND WERE FEARED AMONGST THE COMMUNITY.

MACHETE

POCC

THIS IS THE JACKDAW

WHO HAD THEIR OWN BELIEFS
AND STAYED INDEPENDENT IN BERONA'S WAR.

DUTT

HARI

NEVER WITHOUT
HER GUARDS

THE JACKDAW
ZELLA

REEZ

UNLIKE THE ELE-ALTÁ, WHICH SHARED THE SAME BELIEFS AND
WAY OF LIFE, THE CROPONES WERE DIVIDED INTO GROUPS BASED
ON THEIR DIFFERENCES. LIKE THE CONDYLE, THE JACKDAW IS
ANOTHER EXAMPLE OF A GROUP THAT DIDN'T FIT THE FORMAT
OF THE AVERAGE CROPONE, AND SHOWED IT.

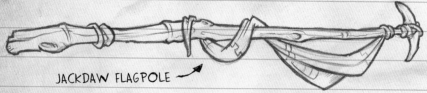

JACKDAW FLAGPOLE →

BUT UNLIKE THE CONDYLE, THE JACKDAW BECAME A PROBLEM
WHEN THE WAR APPROACHED CROPONIA. BECAUSE THEY
WERE ON DIFFERENT SIDES OF THE SOCIAL ORDER, THE JACKDAW
AND CONDYLE NEVER GOT ALONG. SO WHEN WORD OF THE
CONDYLE ENTERING THE WAR REACHED JACKDAW, NOT ONLY
DID THEY REFUSE TO FIGHT, THEY BEGAN CAUSING PROBLEMS FOR
THE OTHER CROPONES. EVEN THOUGH JACKDAW WAS ONLY A
SMALL PART OF CROPONIA, THEIR INFLUENCE WAS WIDESPREAD.

THE JACKDAW LAND WAS LUSH, RICH AND FILLED WITH BEAUTIFUL COLORS. THE DYES THAT COULD BE PRODUCED FROM THE LAND GAVE THE JACKDAW A FEELING OF DOMINANCE. THEY BELIEVED THEMSELVES TO BE BETTER THAN THE AVERAGE CROPONE. MOST JACKDAW DIDN'T EVEN CLASSIFY THEMSELVES AS CROPONES AT ALL.

ZELLA PRIMARY WEAPON

Jackdaw

Lake Debonaire

THEY WERE LED BY HARI [HA-RI]

BELIEVED FLYING CREATURES WERE TO BE HELD ABOVE THE STATUS OF ALL OTHERS.

THEIR PRETENTIOUS SELF WEALTH WAS SHOWN BY WEARING AN INVERTED CROPONE SYMBOL.

ROHT

WHEN THE SHAMAN GOT INVOLVED IN THE WAR, IT WASN'T TO STRIKE OUT AGAINST THE ELE-ALTA, BUT RATHER THE CROPONES FOR PULLING THE CONDYLE INTO THE WAR.

THE SHAMAN REFUSED TO BELIEVE THE CONDYLE ACTUALLY WANTED TO FIGHT IN THE WAR. THEY BELIEVED THE CONDYLE WERE BEING MANIPULATED BY LIES.

THERE WERE MANY DIFFERENT LEVELS OF UNDEAD SOLDIERS RAISED FOR BATTLE.

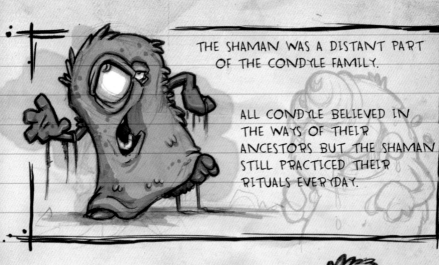

THE SHAMAN WAS A DISTANT PART OF THE CONDYLE FAMILY.

ALL CONDYLE BELIEVED IN THE WAYS OF THEIR ANCESTORS BUT THE SHAMAN STILL PRACTICED THEIR RITUALS EVERYDAY.

SOLDIERS WHO HAD ALREADY FOUGHT AND FALLEN WERE FINDING THEMSELVES FIGHTING AGAIN

BUB- A VERY SPECIAL CASE OF THE UNDEAD.

N

W   E

S

KRITE

CONDYLE

SHAMAN TERRITORY

UN

CO

KR

THESE ARE THE SLAYERS

WHO GAVE PROTECTION
AND WERE NEVER DEFEATED IN BERONA'S WAR.

THE SLAYERS WERE FORMED FOR THE SOLE PURPOSE OF DEFEATING THE SHAMAN AND THEIR WALKING DEAD.

NEVER KNOWING THAT THE UNDEAD'S FOCUS WAS ON THE CROPONES, THE SLAYERS DID THEIR BEST TO ELIMINATE THE DANGER. THE SLAYERS WERE NEVER DEFEATED AND WON THE RESPECT OF BOTH THE ELE-ALTA AND THE CROPONES. THEY BECAME HEROES WITHOUT EVER EVEN REALIZING IT.

THE SLAYERS NEVER HAD A PROBLEM WITH THE CONDYLE, BUT THEY KNEW BY ATTACKING THE SHAMAN THEY WOULD BE WAGING WAR WITH ALL THE CONDYLE. THE CROPONES WERE ALREADY AT ENDS WITH THE JACKDAW, AS WERE THE CONDYLE. THE SLAYERS HATED TO MESS THINGS UP EVEN MORE, BUT SOMETHING HAD TO BE DONE ABOUT THE WALKING DEAD.

BEING A SLAYER WAS IN HER BLOOD. SHE HEARD MANY FASCINATING STORIES PASSED DOWN FROM GENERATIONS BEFORE. SHE WELCOMED THE WAR AS HER FIRST REAL CHANCE TO PROVE HERSELF AS A SLAYER.

JEILAH

ONCE A HOLY SPEAKER, NOW A SLAYER. JUDDIN IS THE BRAINS, BACKBONE AND FOUNDER OF THE TRIO.

JUDDIN

BROT

SMART AND POWERFUL. ONCE A ROCK HAULER, NOW A BRUTE. BROT WAS THE LAST ADDITION TO THE GROUP.

41

THESE ARE THE GLADIATORS

WHO WERE BUT FIVE
AND DOMINATED IN BERONA'S WAR.

HOWITZER

THE GLADIATOR WAS A DIFFERENT BREED OF SOLDIER. EVEN BEFORE THE THOUGHT OF A WAR, THEY WERE FIGHTING AMONGST THEMSELVES FOR "FUN".

THEY WERE THE FIRST TO VOLUNTEER FOR THE FIGHT, NEVER EVEN KNOWING WHAT THE WAR WAS ABOUT.

SECUTOR

XIPHOS

NOT THE SMARTEST OR THE BIGGEST, XIPHOS WAS BY FAR THE MEANEST. HE TOOK DOWN MORE CROPONE SOLDIERS THAN THE REST OF THE GROUP PUT TOGETHER.

FALCATA

GLADIUS

THE CLOSEST THING TO A GLADIATOR FOR THE CROPONES WAS WUBS, WHO COULD NOT WAIT TO CHALLENGE THE GLADIATORS. IT IS UNKNOWN WHO WON OR IF THE BATTLE EVEN TOOK PLACE, BUT IT WAS SOMETHING THAT THEY WERE ALL LOOKING FORWARD TO.

THIS IS BRUTE

WHICH WAS RELEASED IN BATTLE
AND WAS A BAD IDEA FOR BERONA'S WAR.

SOME PLANS SEEM LIKE A GOOD IDEA UNTIL THEY ARE REALIZED. BRUTE COULD NEVER BE CONTROLLED, SO WHY HE WAS RELEASED IS STILL A MYSTERY.

deaths caused by Brute - 14 Ele-Alta

8 Cropones

THIS IS JACUP

WHO LOVED WHAT HE DID
AND LIVED FOR BERONA'S WAR.

EVEN IN TIMES OF WAR, THERE MUST
BE RULES, AND JACUP ENFORCED
THESE RULES.

JACUP WAS A WOODSMAN TURNED EXECUTIONER.

ALTHOUGH YOU COULDN'T SEE HIS FACE, HIS EYES SAID IT
ALL. MANY SAID YOU COULD SEE A TWISTED JOY IN THEM,
BUT A SMALL FEW SWORE ALL THEY SAW WERE THE TEARS
OF SORROW.

THIS IS THE INDIVIDUAL

WHO LOWERED THE BAR
BY MISTREATING MANY IN BERONA'S WAR.

PRISONERS WERE VERY RARELY TAKEN. USUALLY WHEN CAPTURED, A SOLDIER WAS STRIPPED OF ANY EQUIPMENT, WEAPONS AND INFORMATION HE MAY HAVE BEFORE BEING SENT BACK TO THEIR HOME LAND. BUT HOLMES WAS NOT KNOWN FOR FOLLOWING THE RULES. HE WAS CONSIDERED A GENIUS WHEN IT CAME TO SURGERY AND ANATOMY. HE WAS OFTEN REPRIMANDED FOR TAKING HIS EXPERIMENTS TOO FAR.

HOLMES WAS ADDICTED TO PUSHING THE LIMIT ON WHAT COULD BE DONE TO OTHERS.

HOLMES

HOLMES CAPTURED SIX SOLDIERS OVER A SHORT PERIOD OF TIME AND HAD PLANS OF USING THEM FOR LEVERAGE IN FUTURE BATTLES.

OMA WAS HOLMES' RELUCTANT ASSISTANT.

THIS IS THE ARCHER

WHO NEVER STOPPED FIRING
BUT HIT VERY LITTLE IN BERONA'S WAR.

JOEEN WAS BLINDED WHEN A STRAY ARROW SHATTERED
ON A BOULDER NEAR HIS FACE.

JOEEN WAS EASILY THE GREATEST ARCHER THE CROPONES
POSESSED, BUT WAS BLINDED THE SECOND DAY OF COMBAT.
HE COULDN'T JUST STAND AROUND WHILE HIS FELLOW
CROPONES RISKED THEIR LIVES IN BATTLE.

HE WAS POSITIONED IN A REMOTE AREA, POINTED TOWARDS
THE ENEMY AND GIVEN COUNTLESS ARROWS.

THESE ARE THE BROGG

WHO ATTACKED WHAT THEY ATE
AND FED OFTEN IN BERONA'S WAR.

UNFORTUNATELY, WAR DOESN'T JUST AFFECT THOSE WHO CHOOSE TO FIGHT IN IT. THE CREATURES OF THE LAND WERE ALSO VICTIMS OF THIS WAR.

THE BROGG LOVED THE STICKY BERRIES SO MUCH, THEY WOULD ALWAYS DESTROY THE TREES WHILE TRYING TO GET TO THE FRUIT. ONCE THEY REALIZED ONLY A FEW OF THESE TREES REMAINED, THE BROGG BEGAN GUARDING THEM, WAITING FOR THE FRUIT TO FALL.

THE BERRIES BECAME SO SCARCE, THE BROGG WOULD FIGHT TO THE DEATH FOR ONE OR TWO BERRIES. THEIR AGGRESSIVENESS CONTINUED TO GROW OVER TIME.

REALIZING THE POTENTIAL OF THE POWERFUL ANIMALS, THE CROPONES BEGAN GROWING THE BERRIES THEMSELVES. THEY WOULD THROW THE FRUIT AGAINST LARGE WEAPONS AND BLOCKADES, THEN SIT BACK AND WATCH THE BROGG RIP IT APART.

THIS IS THE CREATURE

SMASHING ALL IN HIS PATH
DESTROYING LIVES IN BERONA'S WAR.

PALM CATS WERE ALSO REFERRED TO AS "MOUNTAIN JUMPERS" BECAUSE THEY WERE OFTEN SPOTTED LEAPING FROM CLIFF TO CLIFF.

THE PALM CAT IS ONE OF THE LARGER ANIMALS TO ROAM THE LAND. AFTER SEVERAL FAILED ATTEMPTS TO TAME THE BEAST FOR RIDING PURPOSES, THE ELE-ALTA DECIDED THE BEST USE OF THE PALM CAT WAS TO RELEASE IT IN ONE OF THE CROPONE VILLAGES.

IT'S UNKNOWN WHAT ENRAGED THE PALM CATS AND CAUSED THEM TO DO SO MUCH DAMAGE, BUT AFTER THEIR RAMPAGE THERE WASN'T A WALL LEFT STANDING. THOSE WHO COULDN'T GET TO SAFETY IN TIME WERE EITHER TRAPPED UNDER DEBRIS OR TRAMPLED TO DEATH. AS IF THAT WASN'T ENOUGH, THEY STILL HAD THE ELE-ALTA HUNTERS TO DEAL WITH.

THESE ARE THE HUNTERS

FROM WHICH NO ONE COULD HIDE
AND SOUGHT OUT ALL IN BERONA'S WAR.

ONCE THE PALM CATS' DESTRUCTION SPREAD THROUGHOUT A VILLAGE THE ELI-ALTA WASTED NO TIME CALLING IN THE GRAVEL PITTS.

THE GRAVEL PITT, A CLOSE RELATIVE TO THE BROGG, WAS MUCH EASIER TO TRAIN AND CONTROL. THEY WERE SENT IN TO SNIFF OUT CROPONES AND SECURE THE AREA FOR THE INCOMING ELE-ALTA SOLDIERS.

THE GRAVEL PITT

GRAVEL PITTS WERE MOSTLY USED FOR LABOR, BUT HAD MANY USES IN THE WAR.

SOME SAY THE ONLY THING WORSE THAN THE PITTS
WERE THEIR MASTERS, THE HUNTERS. GRAVEL PITTS WOULD
ONLY ATTACK ON COMMAND, WHICH SEEMED TO BE A
COMMON ORDER FROM THESE HEARTLESS SOLDIERS.

AJAX

THEY SEEMED TO ALMOST GLOAT AT THE
POSITION OF POWER THAT CAME FROM
BEING A GRAVEL PITT HANDLER.

LOUD AND OBNOXIOUS, BLASPHEMY
WAS EVEN FEARED AMONG THE OTHER
HUNTERS. HIS CRUELTY DIDN'T END WITH
THE CROPONES. IT WAS UNLEASHED ON
ANYONE IN HIS PATH.

BLASPHEMY

THESE ARE THE BEAUTIFUL

WHO TURNED MANY HEADS
BEFORE REMOVING THEM IN BERONA'S WAR.

THE FEMALE FIGHTERS WERE INDEED SOMETHING TO BE FEARED ON THE BATTLEFIELD. FOR THE MOST PART, IT WAS THE CROPONE'S FEMALES WHO WOULD TERRIFY THEIR ENEMIES. LIKE A MOTHER DEFENDING HER CHILD, THE CROPONES DEFENDED THEIR LAND.

THE ELE-ALTA WERE NOT KNOWN TO HAVE MANY WOMEN WARRIORS WIELDING A WEAPON. THOUGH THIS WAS NOT IN THEIR NATURE, THERE WERE THE OCCASIONAL FEMALES WHO SLIPPED ONTO THE BATTLEFIELD TO CAUSE THEIR SHARE OF CARNAGE.

CROPONIAN ARCHER

THE BASIC CROPONE FEMALE COULD SHOOT A BOW AS WELL AS ANY MALE BUT IT WAS SOON DISCOVERED THAT WHEN GIVEN A BLADE...THEY COULD WREAK HAVOC LIKE NO ONE COULD HAVE EXPECTED.

JACKDAW ZELLA

THOUGH HARI DIDN'T ALLOW TOO MANY FEMALE WARRIORS IN HER KINGDOM (SHE DIDN'T WANT HER BEAUTY TO BE IN COMPETITION), THE ONES THAT DID BEAR ARMS WERE A FORCE TO BE RECKONED WITH.

CONDLYE WHISP

HANDS DOWN, THE MOST RUTHLESS BEASTS ON THE BATTLEFIELD WERE THE CONDLYE WHISPS. THIS IS SOMETHING THE CONDLYE WARRIOR KNEW ALL TOO WELL, EVEN BEFORE THE WAR BEGAN. THE WHISP, LIKE THE MALE CONDLYE, THOUGHT IT AN HONOR TO DIE ON THE FIELD OF BATTLE.

KRITE SCOUT

FOR THE KRITE, THE LAND IS MORE THAN JUST A PIECE OF REAL-ESTATE...IT IS A PIECE OF THEM! TO DESTROY IT IS TO DESTROY THEIR HISTORY, THEIR LIVELIHOOD, THEIR HOMES. THIS IS WHY THE KRITE FIGHT HARDER THEN MOST SOLDIERS. IT IS SAID THAT A FEMALE FIGHTER IS THE FIRST OF THE KRITE TO DRAW BLOOD IN THE WAR.

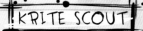

ELE-ELLY

THE ELE-ALTA FEMALE WARRIOR (ELE-ELLY) MIGHT HAVE BEEN FEW AND FAR BETWEEN BUT FINDING ONE THAT SHOWED MERCY TO AN ENEMY WAS ALSO RARE. SOME FEMALE WARRIORS WOULD DISGUISE THEMSELVES TO JOIN THE BATTLE WHILE SOME WOULD DEFY ALL OTHERS BY MAKING THEIR APPEARANCE KNOWN...EITHER WAY, ONCE ENGAGED IN BATTLE, BY THE TIME THE CROPONE DISCOVERED HE WAS FIGHTING A FEMALE...IT WAS TOO LATE.

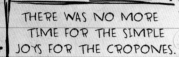

THERE WAS NO MORE
TIME FOR THE SIMPLE
JOYS FOR THE CROPONES.

THESE ARE THE PEASANTS

WHO USED WHAT THEY COULD
AND BECAME THE MILITIA IN BERONA'S WAR.

ONCE THE WAR HAD OFFICIALLY SPREAD INTO THE HEART OF
CROPONIA, THOSE WHO SAID THEY WOULD NEVER FIGHT HAD A
CHANGE OF HEART. IT'S FUNNY WHAT YOU'RE CAPABLE OF
WHEN YOU'RE FACED WITH LOSING EVERYTHING.

NO MORE TIME
FOR RELAXING.

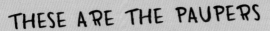

THESE ARE THE PAUPERS

WHO HAD VERY LITTLE
BUT FOUGHT VERY HARD IN BERONA'S WAR.

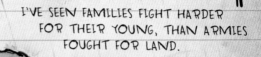

I'VE SEEN FAMILIES FIGHT HARDER
FOR THEIR YOUNG, THAN ARMIES
FOUGHT FOR LAND.

THERE'S A DIFFERENCE BETWEEN FIGHTING BECAUSE YOU'RE
TOLD TO AND FIGHTING BECAUSE YOU HAVE TO.

WHAT AMAZED THE ELE-ALTA MOST WAS THE FACT THAT THE
CROPONES WHO HAD NEXT TO NOTHING WOULD FIGHT EVERY
BIT AS HARD AS THE SOLDIERS TO KEEP WHAT LITTLE THEY HAD.

VIK – WILLING TO FIGHT FOR HIS BOOZE

THIS IS THE GUARD ELITE

WHO NEVER LEFT THEIR POST
BUT NEVER KNEW WHY IN BERONA'S WAR.

WITH CROPONE VILLAGES BEING OVERRUN, CERTAIN AREAS OF THE LAND WERE BEGINNING TO BE GUARDED CAREFULLY. THERE WERE SIX LARGE STONES THAT WERE SPREAD THROUGHOUT THE LAND. EACH ONE WAS GUARDED EVERY SECOND OF THE DAY. MOST DIDN'T KNOW THE REASON WHY, INCLUDING THE GUARD ELITE. ALL THEY KNEW FOR SURE WAS THE STONES WERE TO NEVER BE LEFT UNGUARDED.

HARRIS

THE SPEARS AND HATS OF THE GUARD ELITE WERE DESIGNED WITH SMALL BELLS ATTACHED TO THEM. WHEN A GUARD WAS AT HIS POST HE SHOULD REMAIN SO STILL THAT THE BELLS WOULD REMAIN SILENT. IF ANOTHER GUARD OR SOLDIER HEARD THE BELLS, THEY KNEW THERE WAS TROUBLE.

HALBERD

BRiii

NAGINATA

THE HIGHEST RANK IS REPRESENTED WITH THE SQUARE CREST AS OPPOSED TO THE LESSER OVAL CREST.

IT WAS NOT TOO UNCOMMON FOR AN ELITE GUARD TO BECOME A SNIPER IF HE SO CHOOSES. BOTH THE ELITE GUARD AND THE SNIPERS SHARED THE SAME NECESSARY ABUNDANCE OF PATIENCE.

57

THESE ARE THE YOUNG

WHO WANTED TO MAKE A DIFFERENCE
BUT FROZE IN BERONA'S WAR.

TO SOME, THE BATTLEFIELD SEEMED
LIKE A GLORIOUS PLACE
WHERE HEROES ARE MADE,
BUT HEROES ARE RARE.

ONCE THEY SEND YOU IN, YOUR LEGS FREEZE
STILL AS STONE, YOU CAN'T BREATHE, YOU
WANT NOTHING MORE THAN TO TURN
AND RUN, BUT YOU CAN'T. YOU
CAN BARELY MOVE, SO YOU SIT
THERE AND WAIT. YOU WAIT TO
EITHER BE KILLED OR RESCUED,
BUT YOU WAIT BECAUSE IT'S
YOUR JOB AND WE ALL DO
OUR JOBS. —DEX—

THESE ARE THE INTELLIGENT

WHO MADE GREAT STRIDES
AND ADVANCED BERONA'S WAR.

KRIVANEK

ONCE SCIENTISTS GOT INVOLVED WITH THE ADVANCEMENTS OF EQUIPMENT AND WEAPONS, THE INTELLIGENT MOVEMENT BECAME A RACE BETWEEN THE TWO ARMIES. WHETHER IT WAS DESIGNING NEW ARMOR TO WEAR OR NEW WEAPONS TO FIRE, THE INTELLIGENT WERE QUICKLY ADVANCING THE TECHNOLOGY OF THE WAR.

DAWDLE

THE A.K.

WITH THE INTELLIGENCE WAVE ON THE MOVE, THE NEW ARMOR-KRIOS WAS AMONG THE FIRST TO BE REDESIGNED FOR MORE EFFECTIVE USE IN BATTLE.

WITH THE ORIGINAL ARMOR-KRIOS STILL IN CIRCULATION, TO AVOID ANY CONFUSION, THE NEW ARMOR WAS SIMPLY REFERRED TO AS THE "A.K."

THE ELE-ALTA FOUND THEMSELVES WITH QUITE A FEW SOLDIERS
SIGNING UP FOR THE NEW ARMOR-KRIOS. THIS RUSH
PRESENTED THE NEED FOR A NEW DIVISION OF TRAINING
SOLELY FOR THE A.K. THE A.K. WOULD LATER BE RECOGNIZED
AS THE FIRST SPECIAL TRAINED "TEAM."

—THE WATCHERS—

THE ADVANCEMENTS IN TECHNOLOGY ALSO FOUND THEIR WAY TO ANOTHER IMPORTANT AREA OF THE WAR, THE WATCHERS.

THE CROPONE INTELLIGENT MODIFIED EXISTING EQUIPMENT TO BE MORE USEFUL TO THE WATCHERS.

ELE-TWIN SCOPE

SINCE THE ELE-ALTA TRAVELED IN GROUPS, TWO-IN-ONE WATCHING EQUIPMENT CAME IN HANDY AS WELL.

— MOUNTAIN'S EYE —

TOWERS AND
UNDERGROUND UNITS
WERE DESIGNED BY THE
ELE-ALTA TO ENHANCE
SCOUTING.

EVEN THE ELE-ALTA
ELDERS USED SIGHTING
EQUIPMENT TO HELP
THE CAUSE.

— HEAVY DAMAGE WEAPONS —

SEVERAL WEAPONS WERE QUICKLY ALTERED FOR FASTER USE AND
TO DO MORE DAMAGE.

THE CROPONE GRAND ARROW TURRET (G.A.T.) MADE
SHOOTING MULTIPLE ARROWS EASY.

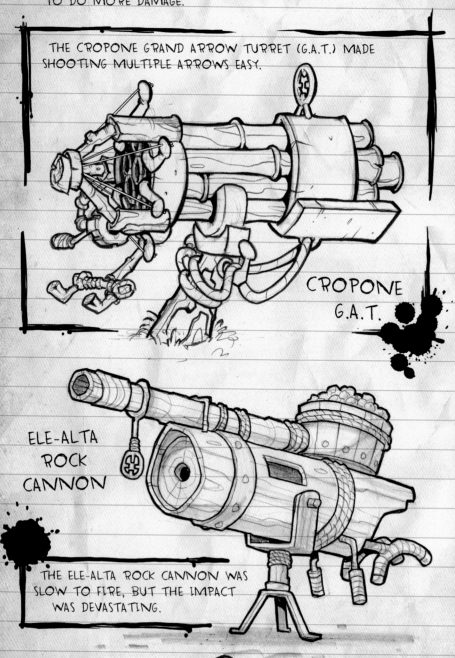

CROPONE
G.A.T.

ELE-ALTA
ROCK
CANNON

THE ELE-ALTA ROCK CANNON WAS
SLOW TO FIRE, BUT THE IMPACT
WAS DEVASTATING.

THIS IS THE COUPLE

THAT MOST CONSIDERED STRANGE
UNTIL THEY ENTERED BERONA'S WAR.

HERO

HERO WAS THE CHIEF DESIGNER OF THEIR
EQUIPMENT AND WEAPONS, BUT CHANA
WAS THE EXPERT WHEN IT CAME
TO USING THEM.

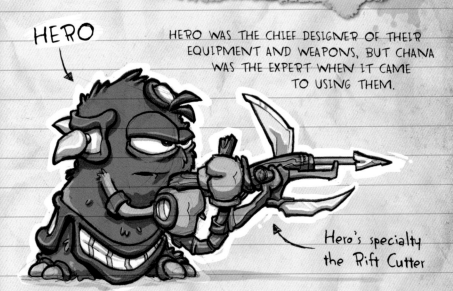

Hero's specialty
the Rift Cutter

THEIR EQUIPMENT AND WEAPONS WERE WAY AHEAD OF THE CURVE
AND BOTH HAD INTENTIONS OF BECOMING KEY PLAYERS IN THE
EVENTS AHEAD.

CHANA

CHANA AND HERO'S
INVENTIONS AND WAY
OF THINKING WERE SO
DIFFERENT FROM THE
OTHER CROPONES THAT
MOST CONSIDERED THEM
OUTCASTS...THAT IS, UNTIL
THE WAR STARTED.

THIS IS A ROCK SLINGER

WHICH WAS HEAVY AND SLOW BUT WAS RUTHLESS IN BERONA'S WAR.

A LOT OF ADVANCEMENTS LEAD TO BIGGER WEAPONS CONTROLLED BY BIGGER CREWS.

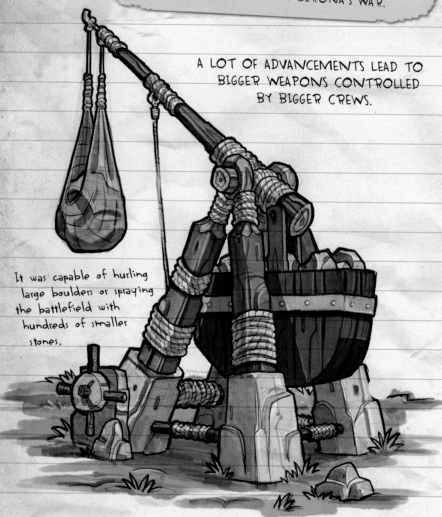

It was capable of hurling large boulders or spraying the battlefield with hundreds of smaller stones.

THE ROCK SLINGER WAS ONE OF THE MORE DANGEROUS WEAPONS USED BY THE ELE-ALTA. ALTHOUGH IT WAS CUMBERSOME, SLOW TO LOAD AND SLOW TO MOVE, THE ROCK SLINGER JUSTIFIED ITSELF BY RAINING DESTRUCTION DOWN ON THE CROPONES.

THE JOB OF THE ROCK
CARRIER WAS A SIMPLE,
BUT TOUGH ONE.
CARRY THE STONES
FROM THE PILE
AND LOAD THEM
ONTO THE
SLING.

ONCE LOADED, THE ELE-ALTA RELEASE CREW WOULD
THEN AIM AND LAUNCH THE DEVASTATING WEAPON
INTO ENEMY TERRITORY.

THIS IS THE TURRETLE

THAT WAS MUCH PROTECTED
AND LEVELED BERONA'S WAR.

THE BULTIN WAS STRONG ENOUGH AND TOUGH
ENOUGH TO GO ALMOST ANYWHERE THE CROPONES
NEEDED. WITH FOOD AND WATER STORAGE UNITS
ON THE TOP AND GRAND ARROW TURRETS MOUNTED
TO THE SIDES, THE CROPONE CREW COULD FIGHT
FROM BEHIND THE BULTIN'S SHELL FOR DAYS.

GRAND ARROW
TURRET

GRAIN & WATER
STORAGE

HIGH HEAT AND CRAMPED CONDITIONS WOULD
MAKE THE BULTIN EXTREMELY UNPLEASANT AFTER A
SHORT PERIOD OF TIME.

KEICREEL GUNNER

DESPITE THEIR COMMANDER'S ORDERS, THE GUNNER TWINS WORE RED TO SHOW RESPECT FOR THE ELE-ALTA SOLDIERS BRAVE ENOUGH TO STAND AGAINST THEM.

BULTIN DRIVER

ANY CREW WHO WORKED THE BULTIN HAD TO BE A CLOSE KNIT TEAM, CONSIDERING THE TIME THEY MUST SPEND TOGETHER UNDER THE UNCOMFORTABLE CONDITIONS.

TAMAEL WHIRLINS

GREGO

KEVCREEL GUNNER

EVERY MEMBER WAS IMPORTANT...RIGHT DOWN TO THE MECHANIC.

THESE ARE THE DRIFTERS

WHO GOT LOST IN THE WOODS
AND MISSED OUT ON BERONA'S WAR.

COVERING NEW TERRITORY CAN BE A DANGEROUS THING
AND GETTING SEPARATED FROM YOUR GROUP CAN BE
EVEN WORSE.

SOLDIERS FEARED THE WORST
WHEN TRAVELLING NEAR NOLLY.

SOME TRIED THEIR ABSOLUTE
BEST TO GET INVOLVED
ANY WAY THEY COULD TO
SUPPORT THE CAUSE...AND
THEN THERE WERE SOME
WHO COULD CARE LESS.

THIS IS THE AREA

WHERE FEW DARE TO ENTER
AND REEKED OF DEATH IN BERONA'S WAR.

AS IF THE WAR WASN'T ENOUGH TO FEAR, NOLLY INDEED WAS. THERE WERE MANY FEARFUL TALES THAT TRAVELED AROUND ABOUT THE SMALL AREA OF LAND CONNECTING JACKDAW TO AMITY. IF FEAR WASN'T ENOUGH TO KEEP EVERYONE OUT OF NOLLY, THEN THE THICK RANCID SMELL WOULD DO THE TRICK.

THERE WERE STORIES OF A BEAUTIFUL SIREN WHO WOULD DEVOUR YOUR SOUL FOR TRESPASSING THROUGH THE LAND. MOST OF THE SOLDIERS FIGURED IT WAS THEIR ENEMY SPREADING RUMORS TO KEEP THE OTHER ARMY OUT OF A NO-MAN'S LAND. REGARDLESS OF WHAT THEY BELIEVED, IT WAS ENOUGH TO KEEP EVERYONE OUT.

THE CAVE OF NOLLY (ALSO KNOWN AS THE CAVE OF THE NANCE) WAS THE CENTER OF THE HORROR STORIES. WHO WOULD BE BRAVE ENOUGH TO TEST THE RUMORS

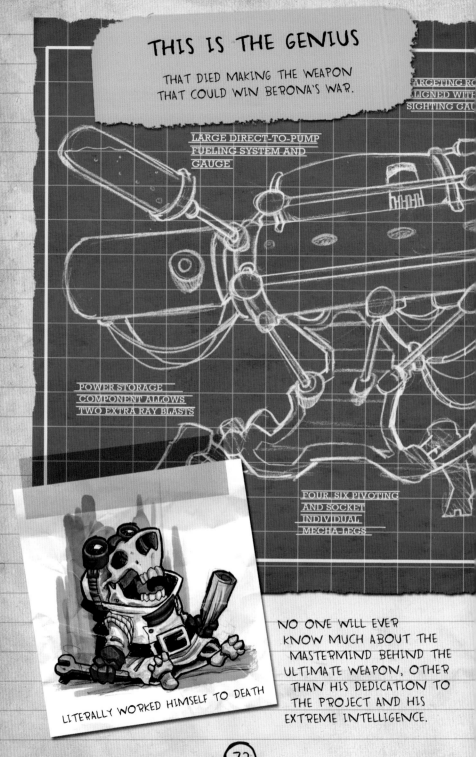

THIS IS THE GENIUS

THAT DIED MAKING THE WEAPON
THAT COULD WIN BERONA'S WAR.

TARGETING RO
ALIGNED WITH
SIGHTING GAU

LARGE DIRECT-TO-PUMP
FUELING SYSTEM AND
GAUGE

POWER STORAGE
COMPONENT ALLOWS
TWO EXTRA RAY BLASTS

FOUR, SIX PIVOTING
AND SOCKET
INDIVIDUAL
MECHA-LEGS

LITERALLY WORKED HIMSELF TO DEATH

NO ONE WILL EVER
KNOW MUCH ABOUT THE
MASTERMIND BEHIND THE
ULTIMATE WEAPON, OTHER
THAN HIS DEDICATION TO
THE PROJECT AND HIS
EXTREME INTELLIGENCE.

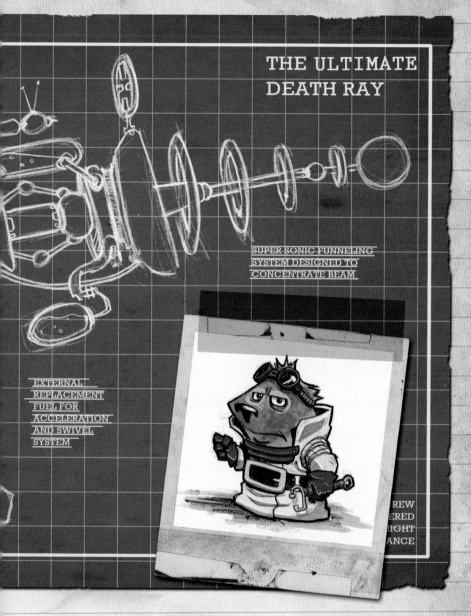

THE ULTIMATE DEATH RAY

SUPER SONIC FUNNELING
SYSTEM DESIGNED TO
CONCENTRATE BEAM

EXTERNAL
REPLACEMENT
FUEL FOR
ACCELERATION
AND SWIVEL
SYSTEM

REW
ERED
IGHT
ANCE

MANY BELIEVED THAT THE UNKNOWN INTELLIGENT WAS
THE ELE-ALTA BAXTER, A FORMER STUDENT OF DAWDLE.
BAXTER WAS DESTINED FOR BIGGER THINGS.

ONE THING IS FOR SURE, WHOEVER THE MASTERMIND
BEHIND THIS CONTRAPTION WAS...HE WAS YEARS AHEAD OF
HIS TIME.

THESE ARE THE SCIENTISTS

WHO WERE BAFFLED BY THE WEAPON
THAT WAS NEVER USED IN BERONA'S WAR.

THERE WASN'T TOO MUCH MORE THEY COULD HAVE
DONE BUT SCRATCH THEIR HEADS AND STARE. THEY
WERE TOO AFRAID TO PUSH ANY BUTTONS.

THE ELE-ALTA INTELLIGENT HAD A HARD TIME UNDERSTANDING THE PLANS THE GENIUS LEFT BEHIND. THE WEAPON WAS TIME CONSUMING TO BUILD, CUMBERSOME TO MOVE AND TOO COMPLEX TO USE.

I GUESS SOME IDEAS CAN BE TOO ADVANCED.

OPERATION "DEATH RAY" WAS PUT ON HOLD BECAUSE IT WAS TAKING UP TOO MUCH OF THE SCIENTISTS' TIME. EVEN IF THE PROJECT HAD BEEN COMPLETED, THE FEAR OF WHAT IT COULD ACTUALLY DO WAS SO GREAT THAT NO ONE DARED TO USE IT.

THIS IS THE CREW

WHO EARNED TONS OF MEDALS
BUT NEVER RETURNED FROM BERONA'S WAR.

THE SAPPHIRE SOLDIERS WERE TRIUMPHANT TIME AND
TIME AGAIN AND WILL BE MISSED BY MANY.

THESE ARE THE RUTHLESS

WHO PILLAGED THE HELPLESS
AND TOOK ADVANTAGE OF BERONA'S WAR.

TIMES CAN BE CRUEL AND THE ELE-ALTA PIRATES DIDN'T HELP.

THEIR CRUELTY DIDN'T STOP WITH THE CROPONES, THEY
TOOK ADVANTAGE OF ANYONE AND EVERYONE.

THESE ARE THE BADGES

THAT WERE WORN BY SOME
WHO FOUGHT IN BERONA'S WAR.

WHETHER IT WAS WORN FOR BRAGGING RIGHTS OR JUST A
REMINDER OF A TRAGIC EVENT, THE AMITY BADGE WAS
WORN BY NUMEROUS SOLDIERS WHO WERE LUCKY ENOUGH TO
HAVE FOUGHT AND SURVIVED IN AMITY.

ELE-ALTA BADGE

ONE RED STONE REPRESENTED
HOW THE ELE-ALTA STOOD AS ONE.

WOOD BONE STONE

CROPONE BADGE

TWO BLUE STONES REPRESENTED THE
SEPARATE MINDSETS OF THE CROPONES.

THOUGH BEAUTIFUL, AMITY WAS A BLOOD BATH AND THE BREEDING
GROUND FOR CHAOS. ALTHOUGH THE BATTLES HAD SPREAD TO SEVERAL
AREAS OF BERONA, AMITY STILL REPRESENTED THE HEART OF THE WAR.
WHILE IN AMITY, IF A SOLDIER WAS IN AN AREA FOR A LONG PERIOD
OF TIME, SOONER OR LATER HE WOULD HAVE SOME DOWN TIME.
SOLDIERS BEGAN TO MAKE NECKLACES FROM THE THREE ELEMENTS
THAT MAKE AMITY SO VALUABLE. THESE NECKLACES BECAME THEIR
BADGES OF HONOR, THEIR BADGES THAT WOULD SAY, "I WAS THERE!"

THESE ARE THE ASSASSINS

THAT WERE VERY WELL TRAINED AND PROVED IT IN BERONA'S WAR.

THE ELE-ALTA ASSASSINS WERE MOSTLY SEEN AT NIGHT, WHEN THEY WERE SEEN AT ALL. THEY GAVE THE CROPONE SOLDIERS A REASON TO FEAR THE SETTING SUN. WATCHERS WERE PUT ON SPECIAL GUARD DUTY TO HOPEFULLY SPOT AN ONCOMING ATTACK.

HOSSIA

THEIR GREED FOR RICHES WAS ONLY SURPASSED BY THEIR LUST FOR BLOOD.

UNLIKE A LOT OF THE TRAINED GROUPS IN THE WAR, THE ASSASSINS WERE NOT AFTER THE RUNNERS, FLAG BEARERS OR LEADERS. THEY TARGETED THE CROPONE SOLDIERS. THEY WOULD WAIT TILL THEY FELL ASLEEP, THEN THEY WOULD STRIKE.

The assassins had to have a dark fur color, so only a select few even had the chance to become one of the silent warriors.

STONE ASSASSINS

SMOKE

THE WEAPONS WERE DESIGNED BY THE ASSASSINS FOR SPECIFIC PURPOSES. THEY COULD USE EACH WEAPON WITHOUT THOUGHT AND KILL WITH EASE...AND THAT'S JUST WHAT THEY DID.

STONE CROSS – A FAVORITE AMONG THE ASSASSINS, THE STONE CROSS WAS AS DEADLY AS ANY LONG RANGE WEAPON IN THE WAR.

THIRD HAND – IT WAS MORE OF A TOOL THAN A WEAPON. THERE WAS VERY LITTLE IT WASN'T USED FOR AND THEREFORE BECAME KNOWN AS THEIR THIRD HAND.

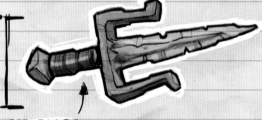

EFF-BLADE – MADE FROM A RAZOR SHARP PIECE OF EFFATOPE, THE EFF-BLADE WAS FRAGILE BUT LETHAL.

THE MAGGOT – A STONE. A ROCK. IN THE HANDS OF AN ASSASSIN IT WOULD BECOME A LETHAL WEAPON.

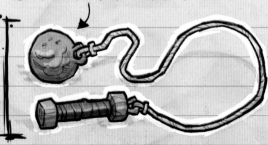

THESE ARE THE KRITE

THAT WERE VERY WELL TRAINED AND PROVED IT IN BERONA'S WAR.

BEFORE THE WAR STARTED, THE KRITE WERE JUST CONSIDERED PEACE LOVING CROPONES THAT LIVED AMONG THE ANIMALS IN THE KRITE FOREST. THEY BELIEVED IN PEACE, NATURE AND THE WAY OF THE ANIMAL. SO NO ONE COULD HAVE IMAGINED THE CARNAGE THAT WAS UNLEASHED WHEN THEY WERE ANGERED.

RABBS

THE KRITE WAS THE CROPONES' ANSWER TO THE ELE-ALTA ASSASSINS.

THE LONGER THE WAR WENT ON, THE MORE OF THE KRITE FOREST IT CONSUMED...THIS WOULD NOT BE TOLERATED.

THOUGH NEIGHBORS, THE KRITE AND CONDYLE SHARED LITTLE IN COMMON WHEN IT CAME TO CULTURE AND LIFESTYLE. BUT UNLIKE THE JACKDAW, THE CONDYLE AND KRITE WERE NOT MAKING THE CROPONES THEIR ENEMIES.

HULT

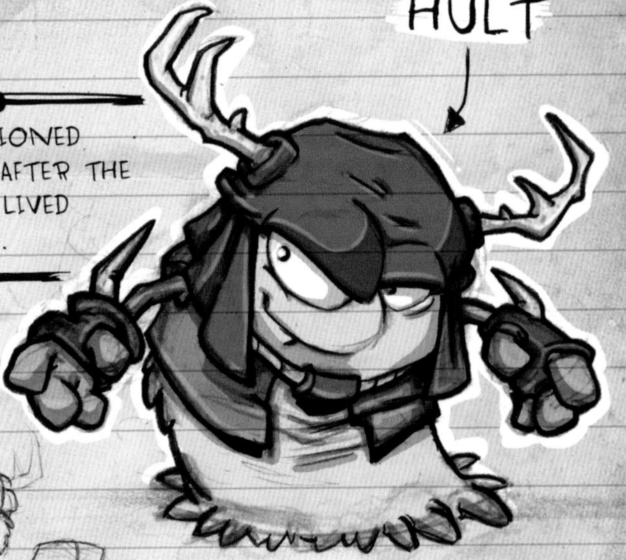

THE KRITE FASHIONED THEIR LIFESTYLE AFTER THE ANIMALS THAT LIVED AMONG THEM.

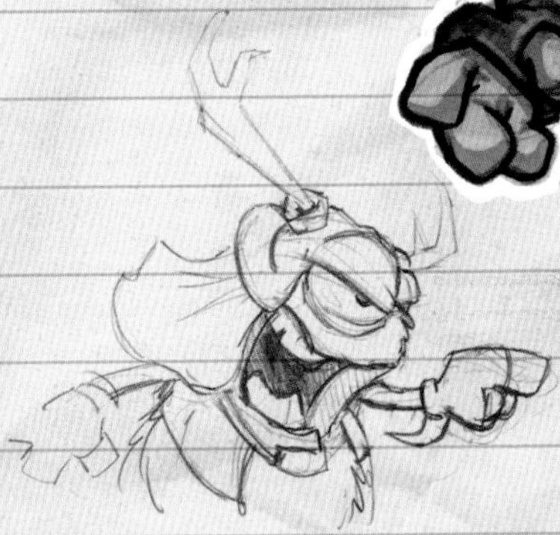

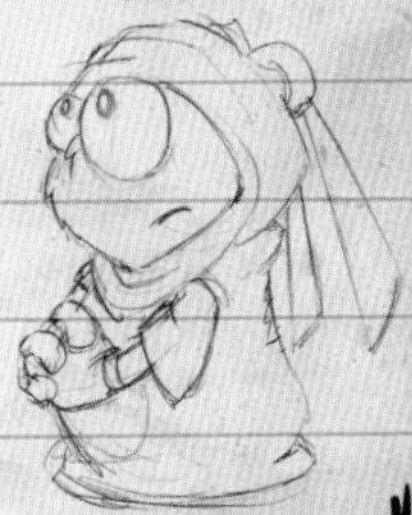

DON'T LET TONNY'S INNOCENT APPEARANCE FOOL YOU. IT'S WELL KNOWN THAT HE IS THE FIERCEST OF THE BUNCH.

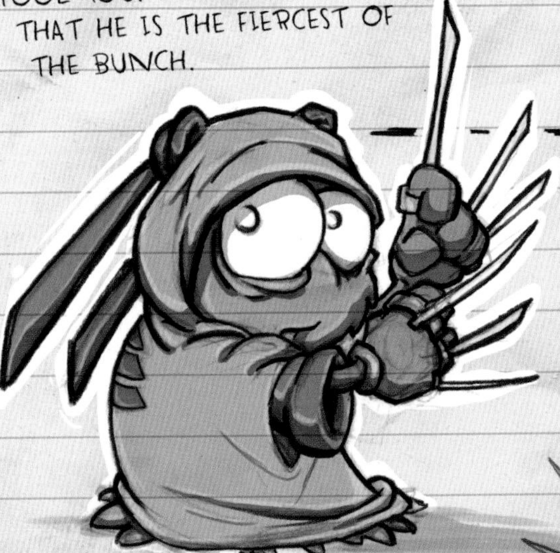

THOUGH I'VE NEVER SEEN HIM IN ACTION, I CAN ONLY IMAGINE HE LOOKS SOMETHING LIKE THIS.

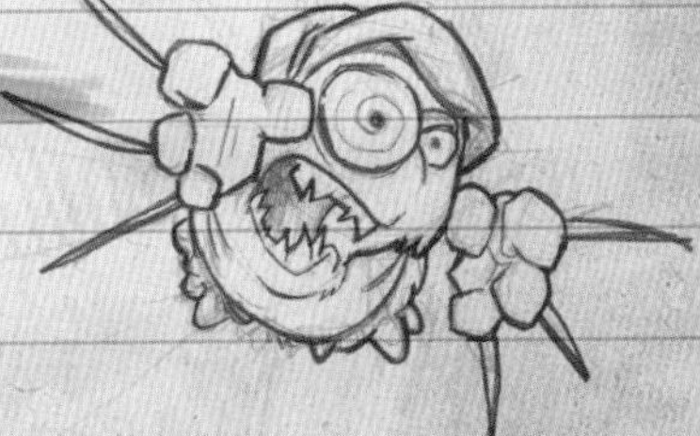

TONNY

THESE ARE THE PROTESTERS

WHO TRIED THEIR BEST
BUT COULD NOT STOP BERONA'S WAR.

NOT ALL THE CROPONES AND ELE-ALTA WANTED TO FIGHT,
NOR DID THEY HATE EACH OTHER.

ONCE THE LAND STARTED TEARING ITSELF APART, FAMILIES
BEGAN TO PULL THEMSELVES TOGETHER.

PURPLE BECAME THE COLOR OF PEACE AND WAS HUNG FROM
WINDOWS AND WORN ON SLEEVES.

THIS IS THE GENERAL

THAT WAS RELUCTANT TO FIGHT BUT HAD NO CHOICE IN BERONA'S WAR.

MANY WHO FOUGHT IN THE WAR HAD VERY LITTLE CONTROL OVER THEIR ACTIONS.

YELL AS HE MAY...HIS CRIES ONLY FALL ON DEAF EARS.

THIS IS THE FLAG BEARER

WHO WAS RESPONSIBLE FOR COUNTLESS DEATHS AND NEVER SAW THE END OF BERONA'S WAR.

THE JOB OF A FLAG BEARER WAS A PROUD ONE BUT IT CAME WITH MANY SLEEPLESS NIGHTS. A WEAPON COULD KILL ONE SOLDIER AT A TIME, WHILE THE FLAG WOULD KILL DOZENS WITH ONE FLICK OF THE WRIST.

RANT'S BODY WAS FOUND WASHED UP ON SHORE.

WHETHER CAPTURING THE HUMOR OR THE DRAMA, FERDI DREW THINGS AS HE SAW THEM.

THIS IS THE ARTIST

WHO SKETCHED EVERYTHING HE SAW AND ARCHIVED BERONA'S WAR.

FERDIE MADE THE DECISION TO RECORD THE TRAVESTY IN THE PAGES OF HIS BOOK RATHER THAN ADDING TO IT.

THE MOMENT THE WAR BEGAN, FERDIE LEFT HOME TO WATCH THE EVENTS UNFOLD WITH HIS OWN EYES. HE MADE IT HIS JOB TO HELP OTHERS SEE THE WAR FOR WHAT IT WAS AND NOT FOR HOW THEY WERE TOLD TO SEE IT.

HE LOGGED ALL THE EVENTS HE WITNESSED IN HIS BOOKS, AS WELL AS THE STORIES TOLD TO HIM BY THE FAMILIES.

FERDIE

ARMED WITH ONLY HIS DRAWING SUPPLIES, HE ENDURED TIMES AS ROUGH AS THE SOLDIERS AROUND HIM.

HE GATHERED UP AS MUCH INFORMATION AND SCRAPS FROM THE SOLDIERS AND THEIR FAMILIES AS HE COULD.

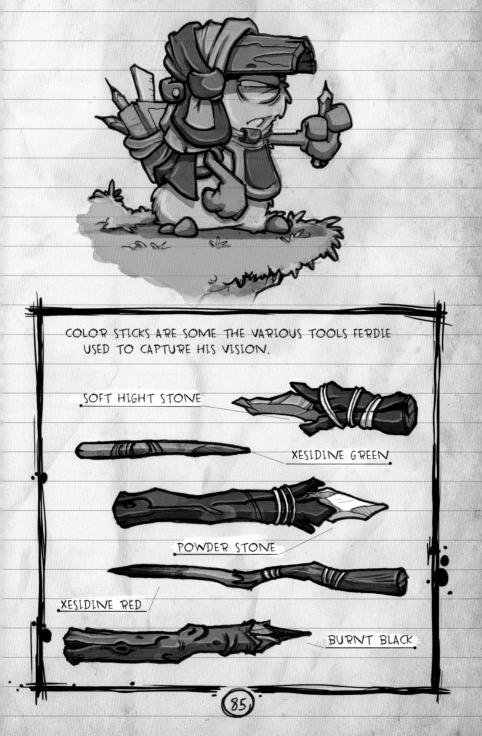

COLOR STICKS ARE SOME THE VARIOUS TOOLS FERDIE USED TO CAPTURE HIS VISION.

SOFT HIGHT STONE

XESIDINE GREEN

POWDER STONE

XESIDINE RED

BURNT BLACK

ROY

THE POET WAS ONCE A SOLDIER WHO REFUSED TO FIGHT. HE
THOUGHT HIS TALENTS WOULD BE BETTER SERVED DOCUMENTING
THE EVENTS OF THE WAR AS OPPOSED TO FIGHTING IN IT.
THERE WERE ALREADY TOO MANY DYING AS IT WAS.

THIS IS THE POET

WHO SAW MORE THAN HE LIKED
BUT CONTINUED TO WRITE IN BERONA'S WAR.

HE LOGGED EVERYTHING DOWN FROM DAY TO DAY AND
FROM EVENT TO EVENT. MOST OF THE WORDS YOU
SEE BEFORE YOU ARE HIS. MAYBE
ONE OF THE GREATEST ELE-ALTA I
EVER HAD THE PRIVILEGE
OF KNOWING.

SOME SUPPLIES USED FOR WRITING

FEATHERS TAKEN FROM THE GINA BIRD
FOUND IN THE NORTHERN POINT
OF ELE-ALTA.

INKING STONES OF
NUMEROUS DIFFERENT
COLORS, SHAPES AND SIZES
WERE CARRIED BY ROY.

THIS WAS THE SCOUT

THAT COVERED MILES AND MILES AND CHARTED BERONA'S WAR.

THIS POOR SOUL MUST HAVE TRAVELED FROM EVERY CORNER OF THE LAND. IF NOT FOR THE ARROW THAT STRUCK HIM DOWN, HE WOULD PROBABLY STILL BE OUT THERE CHARTING THE LAND OF WAR. HE SHOULD REST WELL, FOR HIS MAPS HAVE FALLEN INTO GOOD HANDS.

MAPS HE CARRIED WERE NOT ALL FROM HIS OWN HAND, BUT COLLECTED FROM ALL OVER THE LAND.

THIS IS THE MAP

THAT WAS FOUND BY MISTAKE
AND LED TO HORRIBLE THINGS IN BERONA'S WAR.

ELE-ALTA HOMES

AMITY LAKE

Chana

CROPON

WHILE ON A DIG, M.R. SOLDIERS FOUND A MAP AND A SERIES
OF TUNNELS. A SMALL TEAM WAS SENT TO INVESTIGATE.

THIS IS THE HOLY

WHO CRIED OUT LOUD
BUT WAS NEVER HEARD IN BERONA'S WAR.

THE HOLY

FOR SOME, ALL THEY COULD DO WAS TRY TO REASON. BUT IT CAN BE HARD TO FIND A REASON WHEN LOOKING TO A HIGHER POWER. I FOUND A LOT OF CROPONES HAD LOST THEIR FAITH AND THEN LATER REALIZED IT WAS THE SAME FOR THE ELE-ALTA.

ST. TURNER

MUCH OF THE COMMUNITY WOULD RATHER DIE BY THE HANDS OF A SOLDIER, THAN BECOME ONE.

VULGATE ROBE, HEAD PIECE AND STAFF.

THIS IS THE SQUADRON

WHO LEARNED THE SECRET OF FLIGHT AND STRUCK DOWN ON BERONA'S WAR.

FLIGHT WAS AN IDEA THAT THE ELE-ALTA HAD DABBLED IN FOR QUITE SOME TIME. BUT NOW THAT THE WAR WAS HERE, THE PLANS OF FLIGHT WERE THROWN INTO FULL THROTTLE.

LIVING IN HIGH ELEVATION MADE FIGHT A NATURAL THOUGHT, MAKING IT EASY TO TRAVEL FROM ROCK TO ROCK, AND FROM PEAK TO PEAK. THEY HAD NO IDEA WHAT THEY WERE STARTING WHEN THEY INTRODUCED FLIGHT.

COFFEY

ONCE IN THE AIR, THE FLIGHT SQUADRON COULD SWOOP DOWN AND ATTACK AS WELL AS DROP STONES ON THE CROPONE SOLDERS.

THE FLIGHT SQUADRON WOULD ALSO DROP SUPPLIES TO FELLOW SOLDIERS AS WELL AS PROPAGANDA LEAFLETS ON ENEMY VILLAGES.

FLIGHT-SLING

THE ELE-ALTA FLIGHT DESIGN WAS CLOSE TO PERFECT WHEN JUMPING OFF CLIFFS. HOWEVER WHEN ON LEVEL GROUND, IT HAD ITS PROBLEMS.

IT WOULD TAKE SEVERAL ROCK CARRIERS TO MOVE IT FROM PLACE TO PLACE.

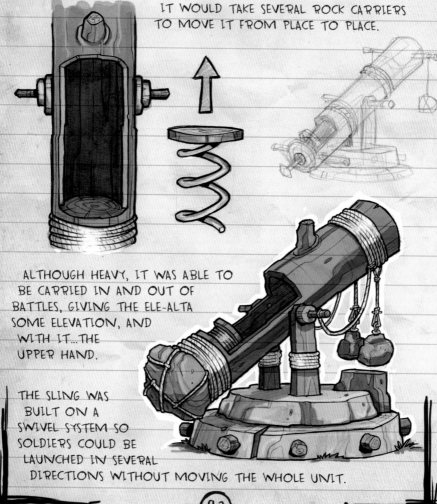

ALTHOUGH HEAVY, IT WAS ABLE TO BE CARRIED IN AND OUT OF BATTLES, GIVING THE ELE-ALTA SOME ELEVATION, AND WITH IT...THE UPPER HAND.

THE SLING WAS BUILT ON A SWIVEL SYSTEM SO SOLDIERS COULD BE LAUNCHED IN SEVERAL DIRECTIONS WITHOUT MOVING THE WHOLE UNIT.

THE FLIGHT SLING WAS THE FIRST REAL
USE OF SPRING POWER AND MADE
FLIGHT POSSIBLE FROM LOW
AREAS.

THIS IS THE SPY

WHO DIDN'T CHOOSE SIDES
AND STOLE IDEAS IN BERONA'S WAR.

SPRING POWER WAS
ABOUT TO CHANGE
EVERYTHING.

THIS IS THE CREW

THAT DID LITTLE FLYING
BUT LOTS OF SCREAMING IN BERONA'S WAR.

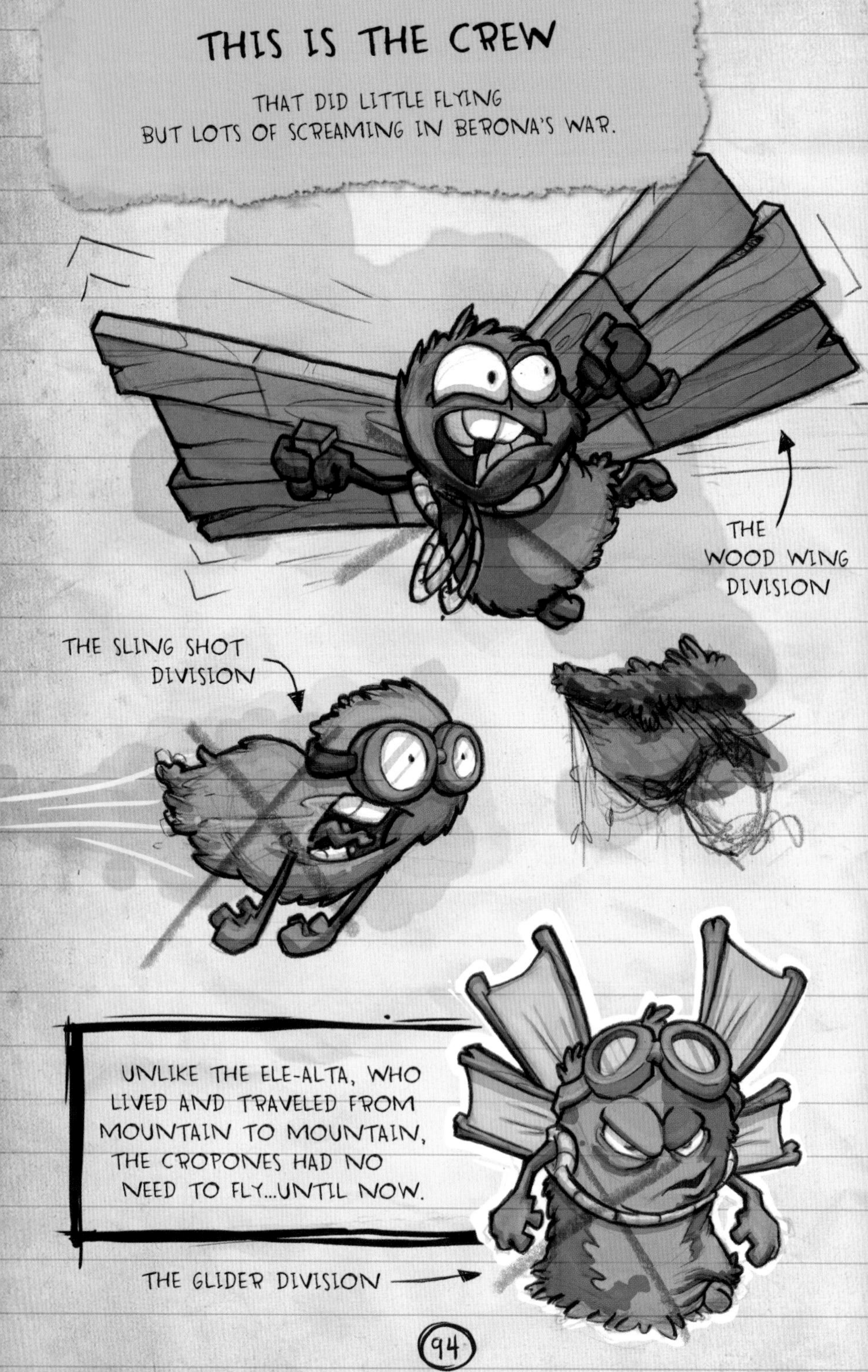
THE WOOD WING DIVISION
THE SLING SHOT DIVISION
THE GLIDER DIVISION

UNLIKE THE ELE-ALTA, WHO LIVED AND TRAVELED FROM MOUNTAIN TO MOUNTAIN, THE CROPONES HAD NO NEED TO FLY...UNTIL NOW.

THE ANTI-FLIGHT CANNON (A.F.C.)
BASICALLY FUNCTIONED THE
SAME AS THE FLIGHT SLING.

THE ANTI-FLIGHT GROUP
SPECIFICALLY DESIGNED
THE A.F.C. TO TAKE
DOWN THE ELE-FLIGHT
SQUADRON.

THESE ARE THE DEVICES

THAT WERE FEARED BY ALL AND DEVASTATED BERONA'S WAR.

AFTER THE SUCCESS OF SPRING POWER IN THE A.F.C., THE POSSIBILITIES WERE ENDLESS.

WITH THE NEW ADVANCEMENTS INTRODUCED INTO THE WAR, BOTH WEAPONS AND EQUIPMENT BECAME FAR MORE DANGEROUS. THE ADVANCEMENTS WOULD CONTINUE TO GROW TO UNIMAGINABLE LEVELS.

WHEN THE DOUBLE BACK CANNON (D.B.C.) FIRST MADE ITS APPEARANCE, THE CROPONES HAD MORE THAN ENOUGH SOLDIERS WILLING TO USE IT. THE STORY IS UNCLEAR TO ME ABOUT WHAT EXACTLY HAPPENED TO ONE OF THE SOLDIERS WHO HAD A DEFECTIVE D.B.C. UNIT. BUT IT'S WELL KNOWN THAT ONCE THE TRAGIC STORY SPREAD, IT WAS NEARLY IMPOSSIBLE TO FIND ANYONE WILLING TO WEAR IT.

-D.B.C. SOLDIER-

FIRED LARGE BUNDLES OF SPLINTERED WOOD

-COJAK-
D.B.C. LEADER

THE DREADED D.B.C. WAS FEARED BY BOTH CROPONE AND ELE-ALTA.

- THE ELE-ALTER -

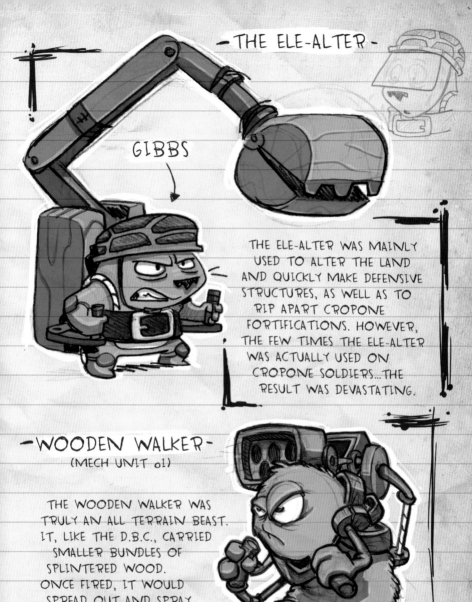

GIBBS

THE ELE-ALTER WAS MAINLY USED TO ALTER THE LAND AND QUICKLY MAKE DEFENSIVE STRUCTURES, AS WELL AS TO RIP APART CROPONE FORTIFICATIONS. HOWEVER, THE FEW TIMES THE ELE-ALTER WAS ACTUALLY USED ON CROPONE SOLDIERS...THE RESULT WAS DEVASTATING.

-WOODEN WALKER-
(MECH UNIT 01)

THE WOODEN WALKER WAS TRULY AN ALL TERRAIN BEAST. IT, LIKE THE D.B.C., CARRIED SMALLER BUNDLES OF SPLINTERED WOOD. ONCE FIRED, IT WOULD SPREAD OUT AND SPRAY ITS TARGET. THERE WERE VERY FEW PLACES THE ELE-ALTA COULD GO THAT THE WOODEN WALKER COULDN'T FOLLOW.

THATCHER
WOODEN WALKERS' FIRST IN COMMAND

THESE ARE THE BRAVE

WHO WERE TOO GREAT TO COUNT AND LEFT THEIR MARK ON BERONA'S WAR.

IT WAS EASY TO FIND A GOOD SOLDIER ON THE FIELD, BUT EVERY NOW AND THEN ONE STANDS OUT AMONG THE REST.

— LUGER —

LUGER CHARGED INTO A GROUP OF ELE-ALTA ARCHERS, TAKING OUT TWO FLAG BEARERS AND COMPLETELY DISRUPTING COMMUNICATIONS... GIVING HIS UNIT THE OPPORTUNITY TO ADVANCE.

THE ELE-ALTA ARE STRONG, BUT THEY DO HAVE THEIR LIMITS. SHELUP CARRIED AN UNIMAGINABLE AMOUNT OF GEAR TO HIS UNIT, WITHOUT WHICH, THEY COULD NOT HAVE PUSHED FORWARD TO BACK UP THEIR FELLOW SOLDIERS.

MOST OF WHAT HE CARRIED WAS SUPPLIES FOR THE MEDICS, FOOD AND SHELTER.

— SHELUP —

– BRUNE "MOMO" MAUSER –

AFTER RETURNING FROM A SECRET MISSION, MOMO MADE CAMP NEAR ELE-ALTA'S HYPOUL, WHERE HE REALIZED THE POSSIBILITIES FOR THE USE OF EFFATOPE. BRINGING THE ROCK TO THE ATTENTION OF THE INTELLIGENT PUT MAUSER'S NAME AMONG THE GREATS.

AS SCARY AS IT MUST HAVE BEEN, DEX LED HIS LINE OF SOLDIERS INTO HARM'S WAY, IN ORDER TO STOP A PACK OF GRAVEL PITTS FROM ENTERING A SMALL VILLAGE. HE WOULD GIVE HIS LIFE TO GIVE OTHERS A FEW MORE MINUTES TO ESCAPE.

– DEX –

— THE CROSSROADS HERO —

WISNESKI, ARMED WITH ONLY ONE WEAPON, HELD HIS
POST FOR MANY DAYS. HE WAITED FOR THE SOLDIERS
WHO WOULD RELIEVE HIM, BUT AFTER SEVERAL DAYS
PASSED, THEY NEVER SHOWED. HE WAS SPOTTED BY THE
ELE-ALTA M.R., BUT THEY NEVER ADVANCED, BELIEVING IT
TO BE A TRAP. HE WAS GUARDING A MAJOR CROSSROAD,
WHERE SPIT WAS TRANSPORTED FROM ONE FORTIFICATION
TO ANOTHER. THEY KNEW THAT THE CROPONES WOULD
NEVER LEAVE JUST ONE SOLDIER TO GUARD SUCH AN
IMPORTANT CROSSROAD. THE PATH WAS SUCCESSFULLY
GUARDED UNTIL HELP ARRIVED...
FOUR DAYS LATE.

THE SPLINTER GUN, WHICH FIRED
COMPRESSED SPLINTERED
WOOD, WAS ALSO USED IN
THE WOODEN WALKER,
AS WELL AS THE D.B.C.

— WISNESKI —

UNDER HEAVY ENEMY FIRE, DOLITON BELIEVED IF HE WOULD
HOLD THE LINE FOR A FEW MORE MINUTES THAT HIS
SOLDIERS WOULD HOLD IT WITH HIM...HE WAS RIGHT.

—DOLITON—

HOLDING THE FRONT LINE CAN BE THE DIFFERENCE
BETWEEN WINNING OR LOSING A BATTLE.

—FOURNET—

FORMER DUNE DOG,
FOURNET WAS
REMOVED FROM
THE SAND SOLDIERS
UNIT BECAUSE OF HIS
GIFT FOR CODE.

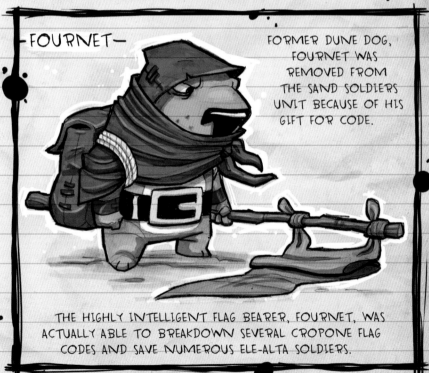

THE HIGHLY INTELLIGENT FLAG BEARER, FOURNET, WAS
ACTUALLY ABLE TO BREAKDOWN SEVERAL CROPONE FLAG
CODES AND SAVE NUMEROUS ELE-ALTA SOLDIERS.

THESE ARE THE SOLDIERS

THAT KNEW THEIR IMPORTANCE
AND HELPED OTHERS IN BERONA'S WAR.

SELF

PULL STICK USED FOR
PULLING THE WOUNDED
SOLDIERS TO SAFETY.

CHIPPLY

MEDICS WERE THE MOST
SELFLESS SOLDIERS THERE WERE.
EVEN THOUGH MOST SOLDIERS
DIDN'T TARGET THE MEDICS,
A LOT OF THEM WERE STILL
WOUNDED IN ACTION.

BECAUSE OF THE AMOUNT
OF GEAR MOST MEDICS HAD
TO CARRY, MOST OF THEM
DIDN'T HAVE ROOM FOR
WEAPONS. THEIR NUMBER
ONE PRIORITY WAS TO
SAVE OTHERS BEFORE THEY
WOULD WORRY ABOUT
SAVING THEMSELVES.

─ MOLE SWEEPER ─

THE ELE-ALTA M.R. WAS DOING MORE DAMAGE THAN THE CROPONE COULD HANDLE. THEY WERE NOT ONLY RELAYING THE CROPONE SOLDIERS' POSITION, BUT ALSO BURROWING TRAPS BENEATH THE SURFACE. AFTER FILLING THE HOLES WITH SPIKES, IT WAS JUST A MATTER OF TIME BEFORE THEY WOULD BE FILLING THEM WITH CROPONES.

ROCK MOLES WERE USED TO SNIFF OUT HOLLOW GROUND, MAKING IT SAFER FOR THE CROPONE SOLDIERS TO TRAVEL.

SEARCHING FOR A SUITABLE MATING DEN, THE ROCK MOLE WOULD MAKE A HIGH-PITCHED SQUEAL ONCE IT SMELLED HOLLOW GROUND.

WOODEN EAR CUPS MADE HEARING THE SQUEAL EASIER.

BRIIN

SEVERAL MOLE SWEEPERS (MS) LOST THEIR LIVES FALLING INTO SPIKED PITS TRYING TO SAVE OTHER SOLDIERS.

THESE ARE THE GRUNTS

THAT HATED THEIR JOBS
BUT WERE IMPORTANT TO BERONA'S WAR.

THE ELE-ALTA WORKER SPENT MOST OF HIS DAY HAULING OBJECTS FROM ONE SPOT TO ANOTHER.

IT WOULD TAKE TWO OR THREE CROPONES TO DO THE JOB OF ONE ELE-ALTA.

-TOOL-

EVERYONE HAS THEIR BAD DAYS...

grain and water
supplier

MOST CROPONE WORKERS CARRIED SMALL
PACKS FOR SUPPLIES ON THEIR BACKS.

DISGRUNTLED STUMP
ARROW CARRIER

A BROWNSMITH WAS A WOODEN WEAPON MAKER.

-PEIN-

THE BROWNSMITH WANTED MORE WORK BEFORE THE WAR BEGAN,
BUT NOW HE BEGS FOR A BREAK. HE SPENDS EVERY WAKING HOUR
AT HIS WORKBENCH.

IT ONLY TAKES ONE

THIS WAS THE PROPAGANDA

THAT SHOWED MANY VIEWS
AND WAS MISLEADING IN BERONA'S WAR.

HOW MANY ARE YOU?

IF YOU HAVE EVER WANTED TO MAKE A DIFFERENCE, NOW'S THE TIME. JOIN THE OTHER CROPONE SOLDIERS TODAY.

WHETHER IT WAS TO MOTIVATE...

RISE

AND RE-ENLIST?

INVOLUNTARY SERVICE IS _NOT_ YOUR DUTY!

...STRIKE FEAR...

107

THEY CARRY MORE THAN JUST MESSAGES

HONER PRIDE TRUTH DIGNITY

HONER PRIDE TRUTH DIGNITY

THEY CARRY HONOR

ELE-ALTA RUNNERS
BE ONE TODAY

...OVER-GLORIFY...

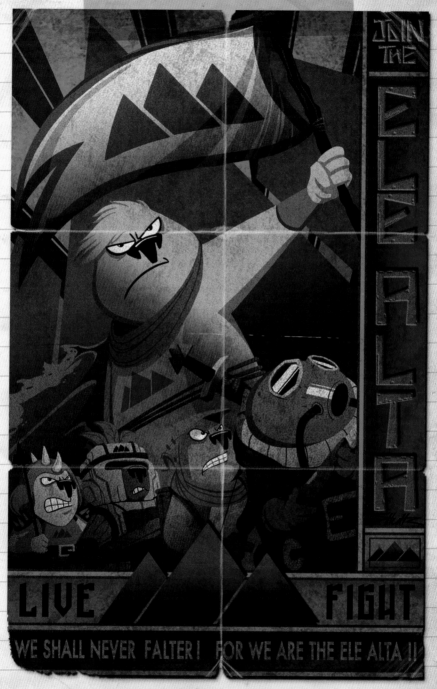

...OR TO MAKE UNTOUCHABLE,
PROPAGANDA WAS AN OVERUSED TOOL.

THESE ARE THE SPECIALISTS

WHO LEARNED THE TRAITS
THAT WOULD PINPOINT BERONA'S WAR.

THE A.K. SOLDIERS WERE SUCH A SUCCESS THAT BOTH THE
ELE-ALTA AND THE CROPONE BEGAN TRAINING SOLDIERS
IN GROUPS TO COMPLETE SPECIFIC TASKS. MOST OF
THESE SPECIAL FORCES BECAME A NIGHTMARE TO FACE.

BAK-O-ROUN
MASTERING THE BOOMERANG, THE BAK-O-ROUN
SOLDIERS USED THE THIN STONE DISKS TO CUT DOWN THEIR
FOES...TWICE

CARLOTA

IKARUS

THE WEST SIDE OTTEG FIGHTERS
THIS IS NOT THE KIND OF SOLDIERS THAT THE
CROPONES WERE LOOKING FOR...THEY WERE
BAD NEWS TO EVERYONE.

PRIEST

MUIR

SCREETS

WATER WARRIORS

DEFENSIVE UNITS SPECIFICALLY FORMED TO STOP THE ELE-ALTA FROM REACHING THE PEARL AND INVERT LAKES.

SOUP

TAT

RABUTE

MORE "TEAMS" STARTED TO FORM AS THEY WERE LEARNING THAT TRAINING AND WORKING TOGETHER MADE FOR A MUCH MORE STRUCTURED UNIT ON THE BATTLEFIELD.

FODDER FIGHTERS WERE USUALLY FIRED FROM THE ROCK SLING INTO WELL DEFENDED ENEMY TERRITORY, FODDER FIGHTERS WERE THE FIRST INTO A BATTLE AND SUFFERED HIGH CASUALTIES.

BLAKELY

SMOOTHBORE

DICTATOR

THIS IS THE NEWB

WHO, DESPITE ALL ODDS, SHOWED NO FEAR IN BERONA'S WAR.

GEWEHR

THERE WERE SO MANY NEW SOLDIERS THAT WERE DISILLUSIONED ABOUT THE DANGERS OF THE WAR. BETWEEN THE PROPAGANDA AND THE STORIES IN THE VILLAGES, VERY FEW KNEW WHAT TO REALLY EXPECT. MANY NEW SOLDIERS FROZE IN FEAR ONCE THEY HAD TO FACE THE DANGERS OF WAR, BUT EVERY NOW AND THEN, A SPECIAL SOLDIER WOULD COME ALONG AND PUT EVERYTHING ON THE LINE AND IMPRESS EVERYONE AROUND HIM.

IT'S BETTER TO DIE TRYING TO SAVE YOUR FRIENDS THAN TO LIVE SAVING YOURSELF.

-SELF

THIS IS THE CARING

WHOSE HEART WAS TOO BIG
AND FREED MANY IN BERONA'S WAR.

AFTER BEING PUT ON POST TO WATCH THE CAPTURED
CROPONES, OMA BEGAN TO HAVE A CHANGE OF HEART. IT
WAS HARD ENOUGH TO BE AWARE OF THE CRIMES BEING
COMMITTED AGAINST THEM, BUT THEN TO BE MADE
RESPONSIBLE FOR KEEPING THEM THERE TO BE PUT TO
DEATH WAS JUST TOO MUCH FOR HIM TO BEAR.

EVERYDAY HE LISTENED TO THE CAPTURED CROPONES TELL
HIM THAT ALL THEY WANTED TO DO WAS END THE WAR.
THIS WAS SOMETHING THEY KNEW THEY COULD DO, BUT
NOT WITHOUT THEIR FREEDOM.

IN THE COVER OF NIGHT, OMA WOULD LEAD THE SULLIED
SIX TO THEIR FREEDOM.

THESE ARE THE TWO

WHO JOINED UP ON THE FIELD
AND SHARED STORIES IN BERONA'S WAR.

ROY AND FERDI MET ON THE BATTLEFIELD AFTER THE
SOLDIERS WERE GONE AND THE SMOKE HAD CLEARED.
SOMETIMES WHEN YOU MEET SOMEONE, YOU JUST
KNOW GREAT THINGS ARE GOING TO HAPPEN.

THEY BOTH BEGAN TO GO THROUGH THE MAPS ROY HAD
FOUND ON A FALLEN SCOUT. BETWEEN THE TWO OF THEM
THEY HAD TRAVELED OVER MOST OF THE ISLAND.

AN INSTANT BOND WAS FORMED AFTER THE TWO BEGAN
COMPARING NOTES, DRAWINGS AND STORIES OF EVERYTHING
THEY SAW.

THIS IS JUST ONE

WHO REFUSED TO FIGHT
AND MADE A DIFFERENCE IN BERONA'S WAR.

IF TAKING A LIFE CAN CHANGE EVERYTHING, THEN SO CAN NOT TAKING ONE.

GRANT

GOING FROM PLANTING CROPS AND RAISING THEIR YOUNG, TO KILLING STRANGERS OVER LAND WAS A BIT TOO MUCH FOR SOME TO HANDLE.

FIGHTING FOR LAND...LAND? IT SEEMED LIKE SUCH A SILLY THING TO DIE FOR. HAS ANYONE EVEN STOPPED TO TAKE A LOOK AROUND? AMITY IS PRETTY MUCH RUINED. I JUST HOPE I LIVE LONG ENOUGH TO SEE THEIR FACES WHEN THEY SEE WHAT THEY ACTUALLY WON.

-WISNESKI-

THESE ARE THE TEAMS

THAT LEARNED TO ADAPT
AND GAVE 'EM HELL IN BERONA'S WAR.

EXTREME CONDITIONS MADE TOUGH TIMES EVEN TOUGHER.
SMALL TEAMS WERE TRAINED TO ENDURE THESE CONDITIONS
AND USE THEM AGAINST THEIR ENEMIES.

THE PEBBLE PATROL

WITH BOTH ARMIES TAKING OVER MORE TERRITORY EVERYDAY,
IT WAS HARD TO KEEP TRACK OF SOLDIERS GETTING BEHIND
ENEMY LINES. THE ELE-ALTA PEBBLE PATROL WAS SENT OUT IN
SMALL GROUPS TO PATROL THE BORDERS AND KEEP A LOOKOUT
FOR ENEMY SOLDIERS.

SOMETHING AS SIMPLE AS THE RAIN
COULD BE USED TO THEIR ADVANTAGE.

COMMUTE SKIS

WEBBON

FROZEN TERRAIN MADE FIGHTING SO DIFFICULT THE CROPONES DEVELOPED A UNIT THAT LEARNED TO USE THE ICY HILLS TO THEIR ADVANTAGE

RATT

BALLTE HALF-SKIS

UNLIKE THE ELE-ALTA, WHO WERE FROM THE COOLER MOUNTAIN AREAS, THE CROPONES WERE NOT USED TO MOVING ABOUT IN THE SNOW AND ICE. AFTER TRAINING, THE ICE TROOPERS WERE MORE THAN READY TO PUT UP A HELL OF A FIGHT.

DELUXE SNIPER RIFLE

JASONEO

THE ICE TROOPERS WERE ONE OF THE LARGER TEAMS ASSEMBLED FOR COMBAT. THEY HAD SEVERAL HEAVY GUNNERS AS WELL AS A SNIPER, A RUNNER AND TWO FLAG BEARERS.

TRIPLE BARRELED STUMP ARROW HAND CANNON

THESE ARE THE SAND SOLDIERS

WHO DID ALL THEY COULD
TO STOP BERONA'S WAR.

MISERY POINT WAS KNOWN AS A HOT SPOT ON BERONA FOR
TWO REASONS: THE TEMPERATURES THERE WERE ALMOST
UNBEARABLE TO BOTH THE ELE-ALTA, WHO WERE USE TO A COOLER
CLIMATE, AS WELL AS THE CROPONES, WHO DIDN'T MIND A CERTAIN
AMOUNT OF HEAT. THE SECOND REASON WAS DUE TO THE FACT
THAT WAR WAS HEAVY IN SOUTHERN AMITY SO SOLDIERS WOULD
CARRY SUPPLIES THROUGH MISERY POINT TO AVOID ENEMY CONTACT.
IT WAS SOON DISCOVERED THAT SOLDIERS WHO ENTERED DID NOT
COME OUT.

IT WAS FIRST BELIEVED THAT THE HARSH CONDITIONS WERE TO
BLAME FOR THE DISAPPEARANCE OF THE SOLDIERS, BUT AFTER A SMALL
GROUP OF SOLDIERS MADE IT OUT ALIVE, THEY REPORTED THAT IT WAS
ACTUALLY A SMALL BAND OF SAND SOLDIERS (A.K.A. DUNE DOGS) USING
THE CONDITIONS TO AMBUSH ALL SOLDIERS THAT ENTERED
MISERY POINT.

EACH RACE BELIEVED IT
WAS THE OTHER DOING
ALL THE DAMAGE. THE
ELE-ATLA SWORE THEY
SPOTTED CROPONE DUNE
DOGS AND THE CROPONES
SAID THEY SAW ELE-ALTA
DUNE DOGS.

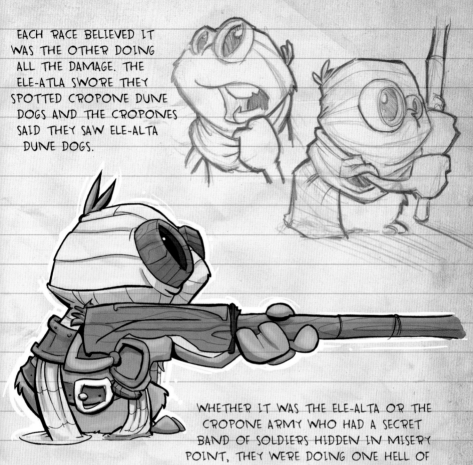

WHETHER IT WAS THE ELE-ALTA OR THE
CROPONE ARMY WHO HAD A SECRET
BAND OF SOLDIERS HIDDEN IN MISERY
POINT, THEY WERE DOING ONE HELL OF
A JOB STOPPING SOLDIERS FROM TRAVELLING THROUGH. EVEN
THOUGH NO ONE COULD AGREE ON WHO WAS ACTUALLY HIDDEN
IN THE HOT SAND ENVIRONMENT, ALL KNEW THEY HAD TO BE
DRIVEN BY PURE DETERMINATION TO TOLERATE SUCH CONDITIONS.

Misery
Point

THIS IS THE DAY

THE JACKDAW MADE THE DECISION
TO COMPLICATE BERONA'S WAR.

NOT ONLY DID THE JACKDAW LOOK DOWN ON THEIR OWN
RACE, THEY CLAIMED THEY WEREN'T EVEN CROPONES. WHETHER
THEY WERE AN AVERAGE CROPONE, KRITE OR ESPECIALLY THE
CONDYLE, HARI AND HER ZELLA WANTED NOTHING TO DO
WITH THEM...BUT NO ONE EXPECTED THEM TO SELLOUT THE
CROPONE SOLDIERS THE WAY THEY DID.

ONCE WORD REACHED THE JACKDAW THAT THE ELE-ALTA
POSSESSED THE ABILITY OF FLIGHT, IT WAS ONLY A MATTER OF
TIME BEFORE HARI WOULD OFFER UP THEIR LAND IN
EXCHANGE FOR THE SECRETS OF FLIGHT. SHE WAS ALSO GIVEN
A GROUP OF SOLDIERS FROM THE ELE-ALTA FLIGHT SQUADRON.

THIS WAS THE PLAN

THAT WAS NEVER EXPECTED
AND DECEIVED MANY IN BERONA'S WAR.

THE ELE-ALTA WERE ABLE TO USE JACKDAW TO SURPRISE
AND EVENTUALLY BLOCK OFF THE CROPONE SOLDIERS. THE
CROPONES NEVER EXPECTED THIS BETRAYAL...AND IT SHOWED.

THE ELE-ALTA WOULD TRAVEL AROUND LAKE DEBONAIR AND
INTO NOLLY. FROM THERE THEY COULD CROSS THE NOLLY
RIVER AND CUT OFF THE CROPONES, TRAPPING THEM
BETWEEN ELE-ALTA AND NORTH AMITY.

TO THE JACKDAW, THE PRICE OF FLIGHT WAS WELL WORTH IT.

THESE ARE THE HELPLESS

THAT WERE CUT OFF
AND STARVED IN BERONA'S WAR.

AT TIMES, ALL YOU COULD DO WAS WAIT.

AFTER BEING CUT OFF, SEVERAL SMALL GROUPS OF CROPONES FOUND THEMSELVES WITHOUT SUPPLIES. THE ELE-ALTA HAD PLACED THEMSELVES IN SUCH A STRATEGIC POSITION, THAT RESCUE WOULD BE NEARLY IMPOSSIBLE.

UNFORTUNATELY, MORE THEN HALF OF THE CROPONES STARVED TO DEATH WAITING FOR THEIR RESCUE.

THESE ARE THE MERCILESS

WHO STOOD THEIR GROUND
AND WERE MALICIOUS IN BERONA'S WAR.

KNOWING THE EXTREMELY POOR CONDITIONS THE CROPONES WERE IN, THE ELE-ALTA CONTINUED TO SEND IN SOLDIERS THROUGH JACKDAW AND NOLLY TO POUND THE CROPONE SOLDIERS MERCILESSLY.

FARCE

RUSE

THE MEANEST OF THESE SOLDIERS WAS A SMALL GROUP CALLED THE STALLIFF. THEY WERE HAND PICKED BY KRAND HIMSELF TO CARRY OUT SPECIAL TASKS THAT WERE ESSENTIAL TO ADVANCING ELE-ALTA'S POSITION IN THE WAR.

THIS IS THE FORCEFUL

WHO DID NOT SLEEP FOR DAYS
BUT WAS RELENTLESS IN BERONA'S WAR.

DARRYNILLIOUS WAS ONE OF THE SOLDIERS INVOLVED IN THE FIRST BATTLE OF THE WAR. HE WAS ONE OF THREE SOLDIERS WHO SURVIVED THE NUMEROUS WAVES OF ATTACKS DELIVERED BY THE ELE-ALTA. AFTER HOLDING OFF AN ELE-ALTA ATTACK FOR THREE DAYS, HE WAS PLACED IN CHARGE OF HIS OWN UNIT OF CROPONE SOLDERS.

DARRYNILLIOUS

DARRYNILLIOUS AND HIS SOLDIERS WERE FORCED TO TAKE THE UNKNOWN PATHS THROUGH THE NOLLY WOODS IN ORDER TO REACH THE SOLDIERS WHO WERE CUT OFF BY THE ELE-ALTA.

THESE ARE THE BROTHERS

WHO FOUGHT BACK TO BACK
AND INSPIRED MANY IN BERONA'S WAR.

BEFORE THIS DAY, THE O'CARROLL BROTHERS WERE JUST TWO
GUYS AMONG A SEA OF SOLDIERS, BUT AFTER THEY STOPPED
COUNTLESS CROPONES FROM REACHING THE STARVING BRIGADE,
THEIR NAMES WOULD BE HONORED FOREVER.

JEROMEY

JOEE

IT WASN'T LONG BEFORE THE CROPONES HAD ALMOST REACHED
THEIR STRANDED SOLDIERS AND THE ELE-ALTA BEGAN TO SCATTER.
JOEE AND JEROMEY STOPPED THE OTHER ELE-ALTA SOLDIERS
FROM ABANDONING THE LINE. THEIR
COURAGE INSPIRED THE FLEEING SOLDIERS
TO STAY AND FIGHT BY THEIR SIDE.

ELE-ESTEEM CROSS

BOTH BROTHERS WERE PROMOTED
AND GIVEN THE ELE-ESTEEM CROSS
FOR THEIR BRAVERY IN THE FACE
OF DANGER. THE CROSS WAS RARELY
GIVEN TO LIVING SOLDIERS.

THIS IS THE CLAN

WHO BROKE THE RULES
AND DID IT THEIR WAY IN BERONA'S WAR.

THIS DIRTY HALF DOZEN WAS ABLE TO TALK THEIR WAY OUT OF
THE ELE-ALTA P.O.W. CAMP WITH THE PROMISE OF ENDING THE
WAR. HOWEVER, THIS WAS NOT AN EMPTY PROMISE JUST TO
ESCAPE, BUT RATHER AN ATTEMPT TO SAVE COUNTLESS LIVES.

MCNOOBERS TRULY BELIEVED THAT HIS TEAM OF MISFITS
COULD END THE WAR A WHOLE LOT SOONER IF THEY WOULD
JUST IGNORE THE "POLITICS" AND GO FOR THE THROAT.

DOUBLE BARREL
COMPRESSED
SPLINTER BUNDLE

MCNOOBERS

MCNOOBER LED THE C.S.S. (CROPONE SULLIED SIX) WHICH WAS
TARGETED BY BOTH THE ELE-ALTA AND THE CROPONES.
THEIR PLAN WAS TO TAKE OUT THE HEAD DECISION MAKERS,
AND EVEN THOUGH OTHERS MIGHT FALL IN THE PROCESS...IT
WOULD SAVE MANY MORE LIVES IN THE LONG RUN.

KOBE

DOOK E. GUN

DOOK WAS ORIGINALLY A MEDIC BUT FOUND OUT IT WAS MORE FUN TO HURT PEOPLE THAN IT WAS TO HELP THEM. BROGG BERRIES WERE ORIGINALLY USED TO TAKE OUT VEHICLES AND LARGE STRUCTURES...THEN DOOK STARTED TARGETING SOLDIERS.

FORMER ELITE GUARD HUTCH LEFT HIS POST TO DO SOME REAL DAMAGE AS THE CSS SNIPER.

HUTCH

RARELY DOES HUTCH TAKE THE TIME TO LOOK DOWN THE BARREL BEFORE SHOOTING. USUALLY, HE JUST SHOOTS FROM THE HIP.

THE LOOSE GANNON IS ALWAYS TESTING HIMSELF, ALWAYS TRYING TO PUSH HIMSELF ONE STEP FURTHER. ORIGINALLY HE WAS WELL ARMORED AND CARRIED A HUGE GUN. NOW ALL HE CARRIES IS A KNIFE...ONE DAY HE MAY DECIDE TO JUST USE HIS BARE HANDS.

THE LOOSE
GANNON

FORMERLY A FRONT LINE ARCHER, OPHER GOT WITH THE TIMES, UPGRADED HIS WEAPON AND LEFT THE FRONT LINES TO JOIN THE C.S.S. HE TOO BELIEVED THAT HE COULD END THE WAR A HELL OF A LOT QUICKER BY TAKING OUT THE RIGHT SOLDIERS.

OPHER

WHAT HE LACKS IN SIZE, HE MORE THAN MAKES UP IN WEAPONS. WHETHER OR NOT HE CAN BE COMPLETELY TRUSTED IS STILL UNKNOWN, BUT ONE THING IS FOR SURE...THANKS TO HIM THE C.S.S. ARE NEVER SHORT ON FIREPOWER.

LAGGIN

FORMERLY AN ELE-ALTA SOLDER AND PERSONAL ASSISTANT TO HOLMES, OMA WAS ONLY TOO HAPPY TO HELP THE CSS END THE WAR SOONER. SOMETIMES A FEW LIVES MUST BE TAKEN IN ORDER FOR MANY LIVES TO BE SAVED.

OMA

THIS WAS THE FRONT LINE

WHICH WAS THE ENVY OF ALL
BUT FELL QUICKLY IN BERONA'S WAR.

SOLDIERS WHO KNEW THEY WOULD BE UP FRONT IN A BATTLE WERE TREATED A LITTLE BETTER. A LOT OF SOLDIERS WANTED THE FAME AND GLORY THAT CAME WITH BEING A FRONTLINE SOLDIER, BUT THE GLORY CAME WITH A COST.

OVER HALF THE SOLDIERS THAT FELL DURING A BATTLE CAME FROM THE FRONT LINES.

THIS IS A LETTER FOUND ON THE BATTLEFIELD NEAR NOLLY.

I FINALLY MADE IT TO THE FRONT. YOU WILL BE SO PROUD OF ME WHEN I RETURN HOME A HERO.

YOUR SON,
   GLAZZY

THESE ARE THE STEEDZ

WHICH WERE TOUGH TO TAME
BUT CHARGED WITH FURY IN BERONA'S WAR.

THE NOLLY STEEDZ WERE DISCOVERED WHEN DARRYNILLIOUS
TOOK A ROUGH PATH THROUGH NOLLY TO SAVE
THE TRAPPED SOLDIERS.

THE STEEDZ WERE TOUGH TO TRAIN BUT WORTH
EVERY BIT OF TROUBLE. ONCE CONTROLLABLE,
THEY MADE TRANSPORTATION EASIER AS
WELL AS BEING THE PERFECT INSTRUMENTS
FOR A FRONT LINE CHARGE.

— TRANT —

LED THE FIRST
CALVARY INTO
BATTLE

HEAD CROUNE

BARCH

A *STOUD COULD BE APPROACHED ONLY WHEN WEARING A
STOUD HEAD CROUNE. THE CROPONES DISCOVERED IT HELPED
THE STEEDZ ACCEPT THEM AS ONE OF THEIR OWN.

THESE ARE THE CANNONS

THAT SPRAYED THE FIELDS
AND PEPPERED MANY IN BERONA'S WAR.

THE ELE-ALTA WANTED AN ANSWER TO THE CROPONE D.B.C. AND THEY FOUND IT IN THE PEPPER CANNON. THE PEPPER CANNON (A.K.A. THE EFF-BOMB) FIRED LARGE CHUNKS OF EFFATOPE.

THE EFF-BOMB WAS MORE ACCURATE AND SAFER TO USE THAN THE D.B.C. THE ONLY ONES WHO FEARED IT WERE THE CROPONES, BECAUSE THE LAST THING THEY WANTED WAS FOR THE ELE-ALTA TO START DROPPING EFF-BOMBS.

BLAKE

EFFATOPE IS A FRAGILE STONE FOUND NEAR HYPOUL. IT WAS VERY POROUS AND EASILY SHATTERED INTO SHARP SHARDS.

ONCE THE EFFATOPE HIT THE GROUND IT WOULD SHATTER AND PEPPER EVERYONE NEARBY.

THIS IS THE CRAZED

WHO WAS NEVER RELEASED
AND GREW ANGRIER DURING BERONA'S WAR.

ONLY THREE LIVING CROPONES KNEW WHO HE WAS AND NO ONE WAS WILLING TO TALK ABOUT HIM. MOST CROPONES BELIEVED HE WAS JUST A MYTH, SOME BELIEVED HE WAS REAL AND OTHERS CHOSE NOT TO THINK OF HIM AT ALL.

WHEN THE IDEA OF RELEASING THE CRAZED CROPONE WAS INTRODUCED TO SRITE, HE NOT ONLY IMMEDIATELY DISMISSED IT, BUT HE ALSO REPRIMANDED THE SOLDIER FOR EVEN MENTIONING IT.

HE WAS SO DANGEROUS THAT IT'S BELIEVED THE FEAR HE CAUSED COULD HAVE WON THE WAR ALONE. BUT ONCE FREE, HOW WOULD THE CROPONES CONTROL HIM ONCE THE WAR WAS OVER?

SOME SAY, AND I AGREE, THE CRAZED IS THE MYSTERIOUS SECRET THAT IS GUARDED BY THE CROPONE GUARD ELITE. THERE ARE SEVERAL ENTRANCES TO THE CAVE...AND SEVERAL POSTS TO GUARD.

THIS IS THE NIGHT

THAT STORIES WERE SHARED
AND THINGS WERE CALM IN BERONA'S WAR.

THROUGHOUT ALL THE ADVANCEMENTS, A RUNNER STILL
HAD TO RUN. BECAUSE OF THIS THEY WERE STILL HIGHLY
TARGETED, BUT NOW WITH DEADLIER WEAPONS. THE
RESPECT THE RUNNERS HAD FOR ONE ANOTHER WAS
IMMEASUREABLE. THE LIFE EXPECTANCY FOR A RUNNER
WAS TWO RUNNERS PER MESSAGE SENT. ONE WOULD
ALMOST ALWAYS FALL.

IT WAS AGAINST THE RULES FOR ELE-ALTA AND CROPONE
RUNNERS TO ASSOCIATE WITH ANOTHER. IT WAS FEARED
THAT VALUABLE INFORMATION WOULD FALL INTO THE
WRONG HANDS. THIS RULE WAS NOT FOLLOWED BY ANY
OF THE RUNNERS.

ON THE RARE OCCASIONS WHEN TWO RUNNERS CROSSED
PATHS, THEY WOULD EACH HOLD UP THEIR RUNNER SYMBOL
IN ONE HAND AND SHOW AN EMPTY PALM WITH THE OTHER.

FROM THERE, FOOD, SHELTER AND STORIES WOULD BE
SHARED. MOST STORIES WERE COMICAL, WHILE OTHERS
WERE TALES OF EXTREME LUCK IN A TOUGH SITUATION.
THEY NEVER ONCE SWAPPED ANY OF THE INFORMATION
THEY CARRIED, NOR DID THEY ASK FOR ANY.

THIS WAS DISCOVERED

AND WAS HIGHLY EXPLOSIVE
MAKING IT PERFECT FOR BERONA'S WAR.

WHILE BURROWING UNDER AMITY, THE M.R. FOUND
SOMETHING THAT WOULD CHANGE THE WAR. A BRIGHT
GREEN LIQUID WAS DISCOVERED DEEP UNDER THE WEST
SIDE OF AMITY LAKE. THE POTENTIAL OF THE LIQUID WAS
SOON TO BE UNLEASHED.

AFTER TAMPERING WITH THE CHEMICAL AND LOSING SEVERAL
M.R. SOLDIERS, THE ELE-ALTA FORMED A SPECIAL DIVISION OF
THE INTELLIGENT, LEAD BY DAWDLE. THEY QUICKLY BEGAN
WORKING ON THE SUB-TERRA PROJECT, LATER KNOWN
AS S.P.I.T.

THE CHEMICAL WAS FAIRLY UNSTABLE, HIGHLY FLAMMABLE
AND DEADLY TO BREATHE. IN SMALL AMOUNTS THE FUMES
WOULD DISORIENT AND TEMPORARILY PARALYZE A SOLDIER
WHILE CAUSING A GREAT AMOUNT OF PAIN. HOWEVER, IF
CONSUMED IN LARGE AMOUNTS, THE S.P.I.T. FUMES WOULD
BEGIN TO LIQUIFY THE ORGANS, MOST OF WHICH WOULD
PROJECT VIOLENTLY FROM THE MOUTH.

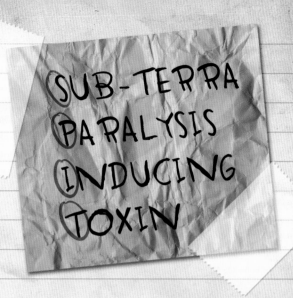

SUB-TERRA PARALYSIS INDUCING TOXIN

ONLY TWO DAYS AFTER DISCOVERING THE S.P.I.T., THE ELE-ALTA THOUGHT IT WAS ODD THAT THE CROPONES WERE ALREADY USING IT AS WELL. ALL EYES FELL ON HASKELL. HE WAS THE ONLY LINK BETWEEN THE TWO RACES AND THEREFORE WOULD BE PUNISHED. KRAND, TURNING TO HIS MAIN HUNTER, WOULD DISPATCH AJAX TO BRING BACK HIS BODY.

AJAX NEVER RETURNED AND NEITHER THE ELE-ALTA NOR THE CROPONES EVER SAW HIM AGAIN.

THESE WERE IMPROVEMENTS

THAT WERE QUICKLY MADE
TO THE WEAPONS IN BERONA'S WAR.

THE DISCOVERY OF S.P.I.T. IS WHEN EVERYONE AGREES THAT THINGS TOOK A TURN FOR THE WORSE. ANY EQUIPMENT THAT COULD BE CONVERTED TO USE SPIT, WAS QUICKLY MODIFIED.

ELE-HAMMER —THE SINGLE L.R.S.R. JR. WAS SLOW TO LOAD BUT COULD DO MASSIVE AMOUNTS OF DAMAGE TO ENEMY STRONGHOLDS.

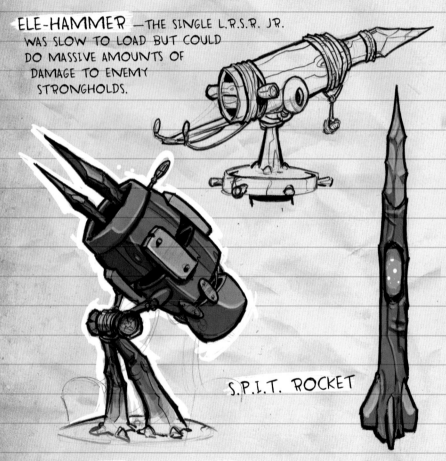

S.P.I.T. ROCKET

CROPONE SIBLING POWER - LAUNCHED TWO L.R.S.R.'S INTO ENEMY TERRITORY. EACH ROCKET WAS A DIFFERENT WEIGHT, GIVING THEM VARYING LANDING ZONES AND THEREFORE DOING A GREATER RANGE OF DAMAGE.

THE LONG RANGE S.P.I.T. ROCKET (L.R.S.R.) WAS USED BY BOTH THE ELE-ALTA AND CROPONE TO DO LARGE AMOUNTS OF DAMAGE TO ENEMY WEAPONS, VEHICLES AND UNSUSPECTING SOLDIERS.

SPIRIT BREAKER — WHEN IT CAME TO THE MODIFIED WEAPONS, THIS WAS THE ELE-ALTA'S PRIDE AND JOY. IT WAS HARD TO LOAD AND SLOW TO AIM, HOWEVER, THE DAMAGE IT CAUSED WAS ABSOLUTELY DEVASTATING. THE CROPONES FEARED THIS WEAPON MOST OF ALL.

SOMMOTET FORCE ROCKET

ONE OF THE NEWLY RECRUITED INTELLIGENT, SOMMOTET, DISCOVERED AN EVEN DEADLIER WAY TO DESIGN THE ROCKET USING EFFATOPE AND S.P.I.T. THE DESIGN WAS PERFECT FOR CAUSING DEATH AND DESTRUCTION.

— OTHER MODIFIED WEAPONS —

THROW STONE

-HICKS-

THROW STONES — ONE OF THE FIRST AND EASIEST MODIFICATIONS WAS PLACING S.P.I.T. INTO SMALL HOLLOW STONES. A PLUG WAS PLACED AT THE TOP OF THE STONE. ONCE THE EFFATOPE STONE WAS THROWN, THE IMPACT WOULD SHATTER IT, EXPOSING THE DEADLY CHEMICAL. THE THROW STONES DIDN'T HOLD ENOUGH S.P.I.T. TO CAUSE SERIOUS DAMAGE, HOWEVER, IT WOULD TEMPORARILY PARALYZE THE VICTIMS LEAVING THEM VULNERABLE TO ENEMY TROOPS.

ELESHRECK

A HIGH IMPACT SHOULDER RIFLE SPECIFICALLY
 CREATED FOR USE AGAINST THE ELE-ALTA
  ROCK SLING. DESIGNED TO
 DESTROY THE SLING AND
TAKE OUT SURROUNDING
 SOLDIERS.

— HARRIS —

NOT AS ACCURATE AS THE ELESHRECK, BUT CAN BE FIRED AT
SAFER DISTANCES. THE SPIT-WAD WAS USED AGAINST SOLDIERS
MORE THAN EQUIPMENT OR VEHICLES. THE SPIT-WAD WAS
FILLED WITH ENOUGH OF THE CHEMICAL TO PARALYZE A SMALL
UNIT OF SOLDIERS.

— PITARRO —

S.P.I.T.-WAD

THESE ARE THE SOLDIERS

WHO USED THE WEAPONS THAT HORRIFIED BERONA'S WAR.

NOW THAT SPECIAL FORCES AND NEWLY UNITED TEAMS WERE IN MOTION, THE NEXT STEP WAS TRAINING SOLDIERS WHO SPECIALIZED IN CHEMICAL WARFARE.

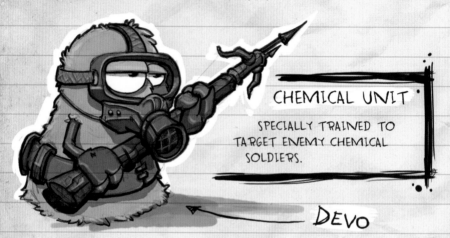

CHEMICAL UNIT

SPECIALLY TRAINED TO TARGET ENEMY CHEMICAL SOLDIERS.

DEVO

THE CROPONE CHEMICAL UNIT USED A CONCENTRATED S.P.I.T. SPRAY, WHICH GAVE THEM SHORT RANGE, BUT THEY DEVASTATED ALL IN THEIR PATH.

COOK

THE COOKS WERE USED TO TORCH ENEMY SOLDIERS AND EQUIPMENT.

CHASE

CHEMICAL SOLDIERS WERE HIGHLY FEARED BECAUSE EVERYONE
KNEW WHAT THEY WERE CAPABLE OF.

THE ELE-ALTA CHEMICAL TROOPERS USED THE S.P.I.T. "FUMES"
WHICH COVERED MORE GROUND AND MADE ANY SORT OF
ENEMY ADVANCEMENT NEAR IMPOSSIBLE.

CRYST

BUNKER BLASTER

USED TO CLEAR ENEMY TRENCHES
AND ENCLOSED STRONGHOLDS.

DEVIL'S BREATH

SPREADS FUMES OVER LARGE
AREAS AND ALSO REPELS
ENEMY CHEMICAL SPRAY.

NOAH

THESE ARE THE LOYAL

WHO MADE IT A POINT TO RECLAIM BERONA'S WAR.

THE TIME HAD COME THAT MANY CONDYLE HAD BEEN WAITING FOR. IT WAS NO SECRET THAT THERE WAS NO LOVE BETWEEN THE JACKDAW AND THE CONDYLE, SO WHEN THE CHANCE FOR VENGEANCE WAS GIVEN TO THE CONDYLE WARRIORS, THEY WERE MORE THAN HAPPY TO JOIN A SMALL UNIT OF CROPONES TO RETAKE THE LAND THAT THE JACKDAW HANDED OVER TO THE ENEMY, AS WELL AS SHOW THEM THE PRICE THAT IS PAID FOR TREASON.

FORMER WATCHER POWELL, WAS PLACED IN CHARGE OF 13 CROPONES INCLUDING 9 CONDYLE.

POWELL

THE CROPONES HAD THEIR HANDS FULL WITH THE ELE-ALTA BUT SOMETHING HAD TO BE DONE ABOUT THE JACKDAW SELLING OUT THEIR OWN RACE. A SMALL GROUP OF CROPONES, WITH THE HELP OF THE CONDYLE, WOULD SUIT UP AND TAKE BACK WHAT THEY BELIEVED WAS THEIRS.

HIS RANK FELL RIGHT UNDER CONDYLE LEADER ASSAM. HE
WAS NOW IN CHARGE OF KEEPING THE OTHER CONDYLE IN
LINE...SOMETHING THAT THEY WERE NOT FAMILIAR WITH.

MCPHAIL

AFTER DECIDING TO JOIN THE UNIT, THE
CONDYLE REFUSED TO LOSE THEIR MASKS
OR THEIR CULTURE. A COMPROMISE
WAS MADE AND THE NEW CHEMICAL
CONDYLE WERE FORMED.

THE
CHEMICAL CONDYLE

IF THINGS WENT ACCORDING TO PLAN, THE JACKDAW WOULD
NEVER INTERFERE AGAIN.

THESE ARE THE MOURNFUL

WHO SAW FRIENDS AND FAMILY FALL
AND WILL NEVER FORGET BERONA'S WAR.

WHAT
YOU'VE SEEN...

...CAN NEVER BE UN-SEEN.

THESE ARE THE ROOKIES

WHO KNEW VERY LITTLE
AND DISAPPEARED IN BERONA'S WAR.

WITH THE PACE OF THE WAR INCREASING, MANY SOLDIERS WERE THROWN INTO THE BATTLE WITHOUT PROPER TRAINING. SOMETIMES ROOKIES TRIED TOO HARD TO BE NOTICED, SOMETIMES ORDERS ARE MISUNDERSTOOD AND SOMETIMES...SOLDIERS JUST AREN'T THINKING.

THESE ARE THE RECRUITS

WHO WILL REPLACE THE FALLEN AND FOLLOW SUIT IN BERONA'S WAR.

SOLDIERS FALL FAST SO THEY MUST ALSO BE REPLACED FAST.

CROPONE ADVANCED TRAINEES

SOLDIERS ARE ALL TOO EASY TO REPLACE. THERE IS ALWAYS SOMEONE WHO WANTS TO BE THE HERO, SOMEONE WHO WANTS TO FOLLOW IN THE FOOTSTEPS OF ANOTHER OR SOMEONE WHO CAN BE PERSUADED.

EBBAL

THERE'S ALWAYS SOMEONE TO CONTINUE THE WAR.

THE ELE-YOUTH

WHEN ASKED, MOST SOLDIERS WEREN'T EVEN ABLE TO
REMEMBER WHAT STARTED ALL THE FIGHTING. EACH SIDE
JUST BLAMED THE OTHER.

THIS WAS THE CATASTROPHE

THAT LIT UP THE SKY
AND IMPACTED ALL IN BERONA'S WAR.

AFTER THEIR SCIENTISTS STUMBLED UPON THE EXPLOSIVE NATURE OF S.P.I.T., THE ELE-ALTA FOUND THEMSELVES IN A RACE TO STOP THE EXCAVATION OF AMITY MOUNTAIN, WHERE A RIVER OF THE VOLATILE SUBSTANCE HAD REPORTEDLY BEEN DISCOVERED. THE TOP SECRET NATURE OF THE TUNNELING OPERATION, COUPLED WITH A MASSIVE MOBILIZATION OF CROPONE TROOPS SURROUNDING THE MOUNTAIN, DOOMED ALL ATTEMPTS TO GET A MESSAGE THROUGH IN TIME.

BEFORE THE CATASTROPHE, SOME STILL BELIEVED THE WAR WOULD BE A SHORT-LIVED CONFLICT, BUT AFTER THE SKY TURNED WHITE FEW THOUGHT THEY WOULD SEE ITS END. NO ONE COULD HAVE KNOWN THAT THIS TRAGEDY WOULD LATER IMPACT THE WORLD OF BERONA IN AN EVEN GREATER AND MORE TERRIFYING WAY.

THESE ARE THE LEADERS

WHO WERE CONSUMED BY GREED
AND CONTINUED BERONA'S WAR.

IF YOU CLIMB THE LADDER HIGH ENOUGH, YOU WILL
EVENTUALLY FIND THE ONES RESPONSIBLE.

KRAND WAS HELL-BENT ON
GETTING WHAT HE WANTED
AND SINCE HE HAD YET TO
LOSE ANYTHING HE CARED
ABOUT, HE WOULD
CONTINUE THROWING
EVERYTHING HE HAD AT
THE CROPONES.

SRITE HAD LOST SEVERAL
FRIENDS AFTER SENDING THEM
TO THE FRONT LINE, SO AT
THIS POINT LETTING THE WAR
GO WOULD BE A WASTE OF
THEIR LIVES. NEVER STOPPING
TO THINK ABOUT THE LIVES
THAT WOULD CONTINUE TO
BE LOST, HE WOULD NOT
STOP UNTIL AMITY BELONGED
TO THE CROPONES.

THE CLOSEST THESE TWO EVER CAME TO THE BATTLE WAS
IN THE STORIES THEY HEARD.

AMITY...WHAT A WONDERFUL NAME.

(151)

BROTHERS WHO GREW UP TOGETHER...HAVE NOW FALLEN TOGETHER.

BEST FRIENDS REFUSED TO
LEAVE EACH OTHERS SIDE.

WAR IS EXPENSIVE...

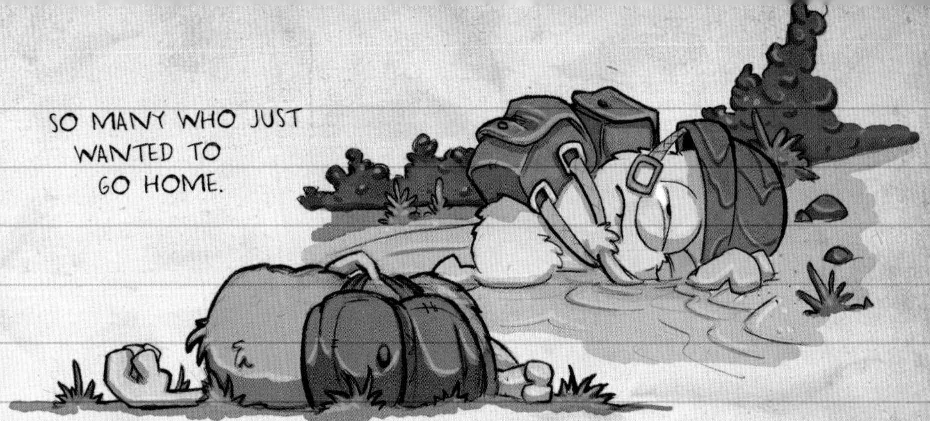
SO MANY WHO JUST WANTED TO GO HOME.

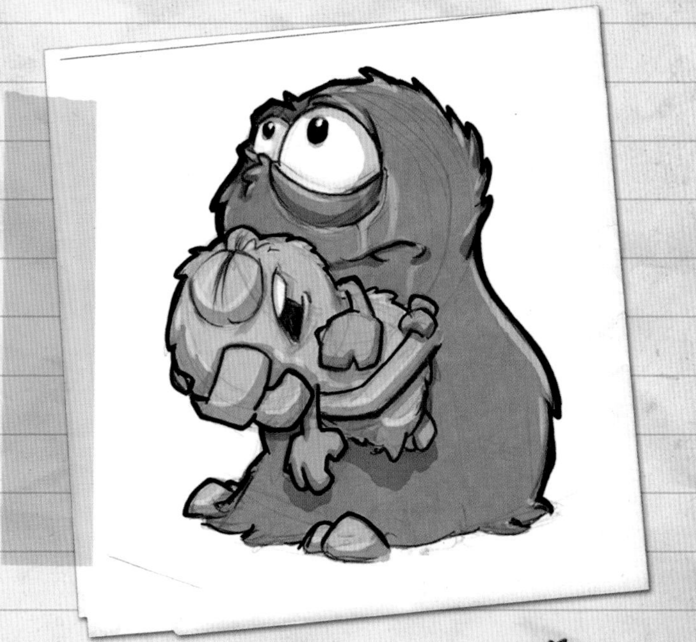

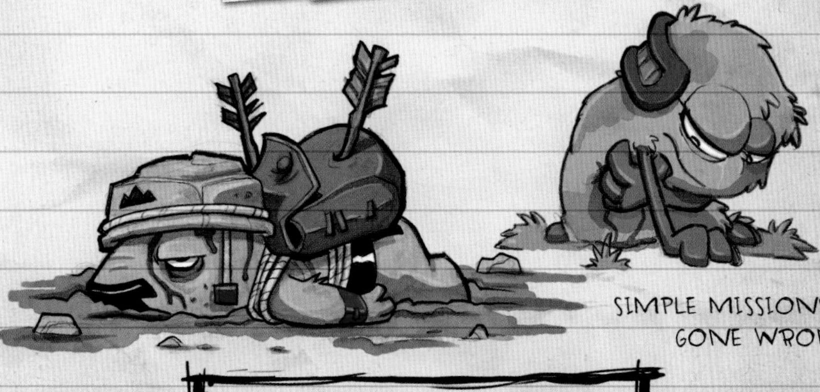
SIMPLE MISSIONS GONE WRONG.

...AND EVERYONE PAYS FOR IT.

BERONA'S WAR

AMITY WAS ONCE A PLACE WHERE THE GREEN MET THE GREY...BUT NOW IT'S ONLY A PLACE WHERE BLOOD MEETS DIRT, A WASTELAND THAT NO ONE WOULD WANT. YET THE BATTLE FOR IT RAGES ON.

AS CHILDREN WE WERE TAUGHT TO HATE OUR NEIGHBORS BECAUSE THEY WERE TRYING TO TAKE THAT WHICH WAS RIGHTFULLY OURS. WE WERE TAUGHT THAT WE HAD NOTHING IN COMMON WITH THESE MONSTERS BUT A HATRED FOR EACH OTHER. THEN WE MET, AND LEARNED THAT ALL WE HAD BEEN TAUGHT WAS NOT ONLY WRONG, BUT UTTERLY INSANE. BY THEN, WE HAD LOST OUR FAMILIES, FRIENDS AND HOMES. WHAT'S MORE, WE HAD LOST HOPE. HOPE THAT THERE WOULD BE SOME PURPOSE...SOME JUSTIFICATION BEHIND THIS INSANITY. OUR TWO RACES FIGHT TO OWN A LAND THAT BELONGED TO NEITHER OF THEM. LAND THAT, IF IT COULD, WOULD DISOWN US ALL. BUT THE LAND CANNOT SPEAK...SO WE WILL SPEAK FOR IT.

MY NAME IS BERONA
AND THIS IS MY WAR.

ROY   ME   FERDIE

WITH HOPE
LYNN

THE END

WHY?

IT COULD BE EASY TO THINK THE INSPIRATION BEHIND THIS BOOK WAS A (PERHAPS TWISTED) FASCINATION WITH WAR, OR EVEN A (PERHAPS CHEESY) ATTEMPT AT SOME ANTI-WAR SENTIMENT. BUT NO...THE TRUTH IS FAR LESS TWISTED, BUT PERHAPS JUST AS CHEESY, OR CHILDISH, TO BE MORE ACCURATE. TRUTH BE KNOWN, WE JUST WANTED TO HAVE A LITTLE FUN.

WE HOPE YOU ENJOYED OUR BOOK. WE INDEED HAD A GOOD TIME PUTTING IT TOGETHER. WE TRIED TO CAPTURE AS MUCH FUN AS WE COULD FROM OUR CHILDHOOD WHILE WORKING ON BERONA'S WAR. IT'S ALWAYS FUN TO LOOK BACK IN OUR PAST TO THAT SPECIAL PART OF OUR MEMORIES WHEN SATURDAY MORNING CARTOONS ONLY PLAYED ON SATURDAY MORNINGS, AS OPPOSED TO EVERYDAY! THE PART THAT USE TO MEMORIZE THE BIO CARDS FOR ALL OF OUR G.I. JOE AND TRANSFORMERS. THE TIMES SPENT PLAYING IN THE BACK YARD, DIGGING LITTLE FOXHOLES AND BUILDING FORTRESSES FOR THE TONS OF ARMY MEN WE OWNED.

NOWADAYS, IF YOU WERE TO GIVE A KID ONE OF YOUR MOST CHERISHED CHILDHOOD TOYS THE FIRST THING OUT OF THEIR MOUTHS WOULD BE, "WHAT DOES IT DO?" EITHER THAT OR THEY BEGIN LOOKING FOR THE USB PORTS. WELL I'LL TELL YOU WHAT IT DOES KID, "IT MAKES YOU USE YOUR IMAGINATION!"

WE HAVE PURPOSELY SET UP THIS BOOK AND ITS CHARACTERS TO BE OPEN-ENDED. WE GAVE THEM JUST ENOUGH PERSONALITY THAT THEIR PATHS CAN CONTINUE IN ANY DIRECTION YOU CHOOSE. WE HAVE PLANS FOR BERONA AND ALL ITS CREATURES AND SINCE WE SEEM TO BE TOO OLD TO GO AND PLAY OUTSIDE...BERONA HAS BECOME OUR SANDBOX AND THESE ARE OUR ARMY MEN.

IF SOME OF THESE CHARACTERS LOOKED FAMILIAR, THIS MIGHT BE WHY...

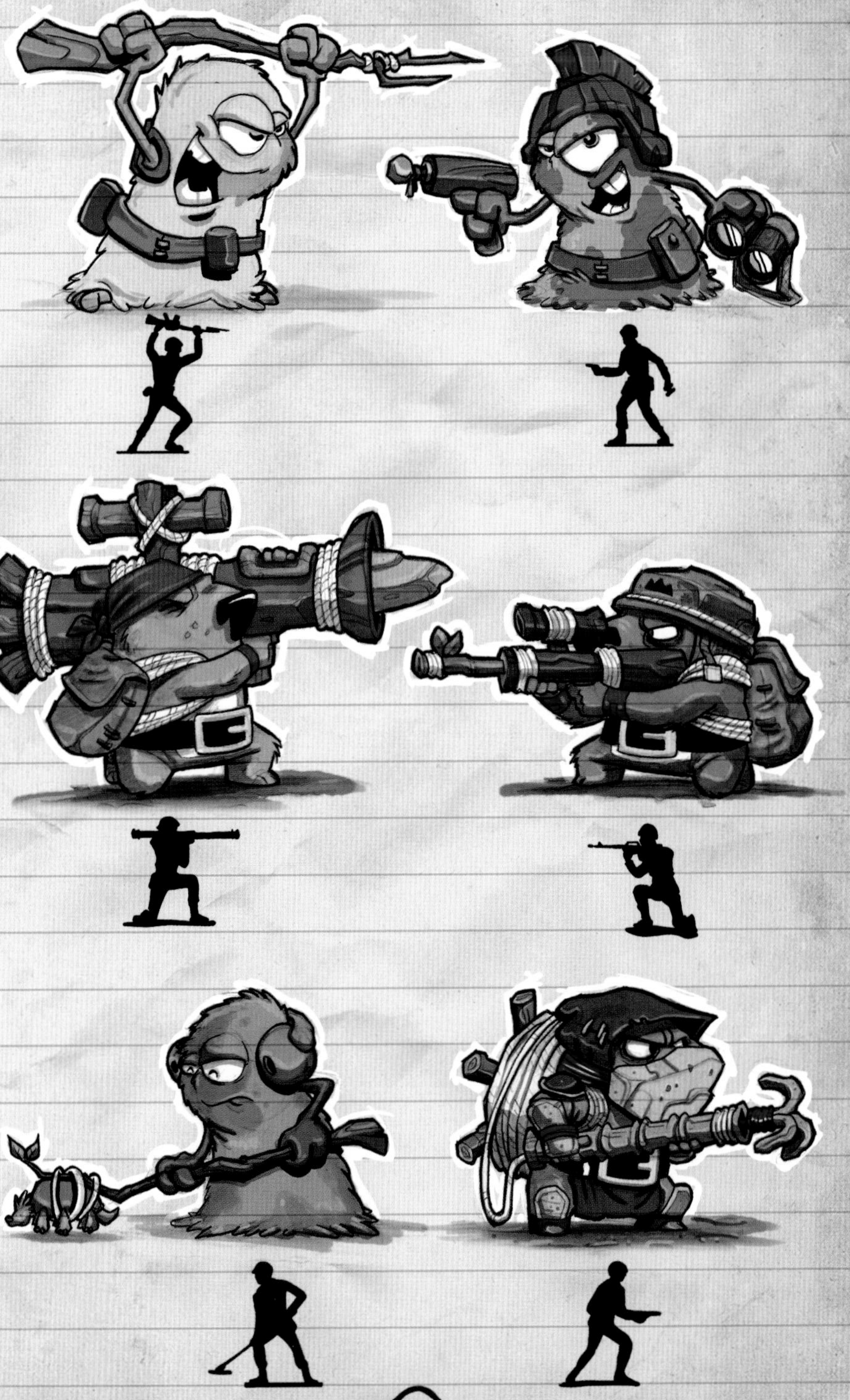

THIS WAR HAS BEEN SUPPLIED BY HEROES AND DREAMS. WITHOUT THEIR LOVE AND SUPPORT THERE MAY NEVER HAVE BEEN ANY BLOODSHED, VIOLENCE OR UNNECESSARY DEATHS OF FRIENDS AND LOVED ONES...THANKS A BUNCH, HEROES AND DREAMS!

JAY

ACTUALLY HEROES AND DREAMS HAS BEEN VERY SUPPORTIVE THROUGHOUT THE MAKING OF THIS BOOK. SO TO JAY, DALE AND ALL THEIR EMPLOYEES...THANK YOU.

WWW.HEROESANDDREAMS.COM

WWW.MYSPACE.COM/HEROESANDDREAMSCOMICS

HTTP://WWW.FACEBOOK.COM/JAYLONG.HEROESANDDREAMS

HTTP://TWITTER.COM/HEROESANDDREAMS

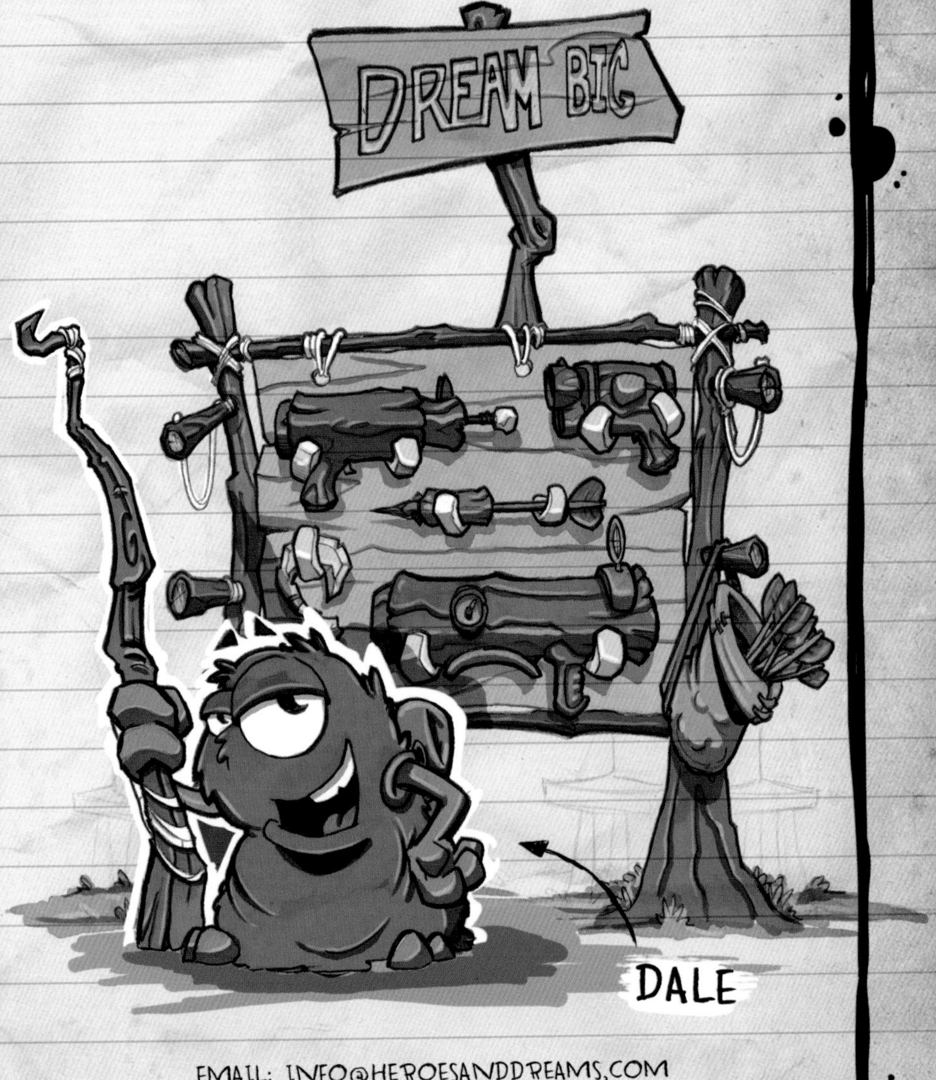
DREAM BIG
DALE

EMAIL: INFO@HEROESANDDREAMS,COM

PHONE: 601-992-3100

ITS WHY WE FEAR THE WATER...